Celebrating the Welsh Princes

Elin Meek

Translated by Siân Lewis

GWASG CARREG GWALCH

The Royal Houses of Wales

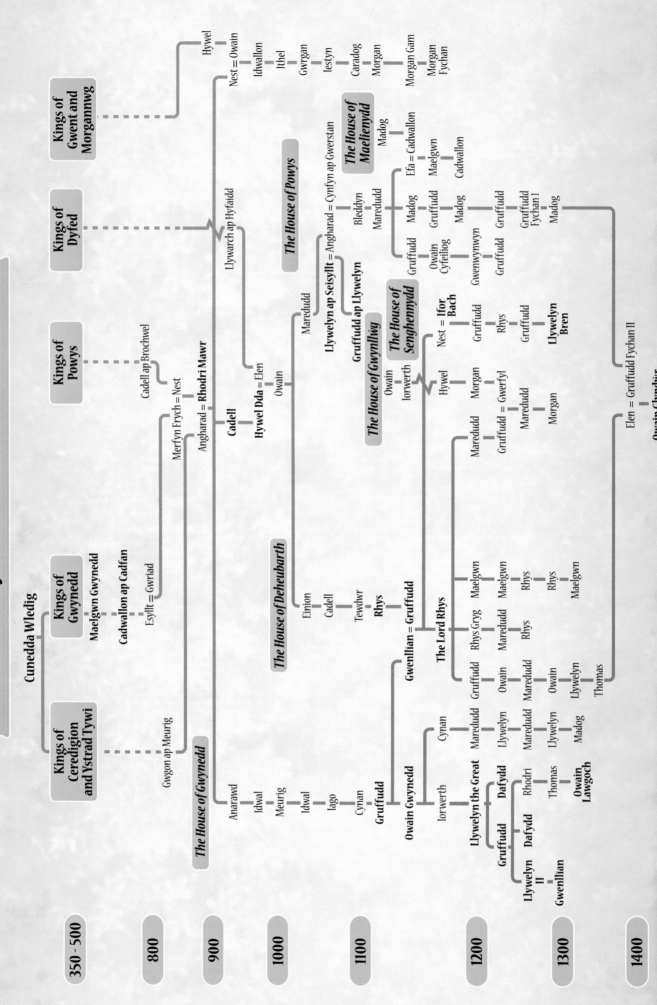

Contents

How the Members of a Family are Related

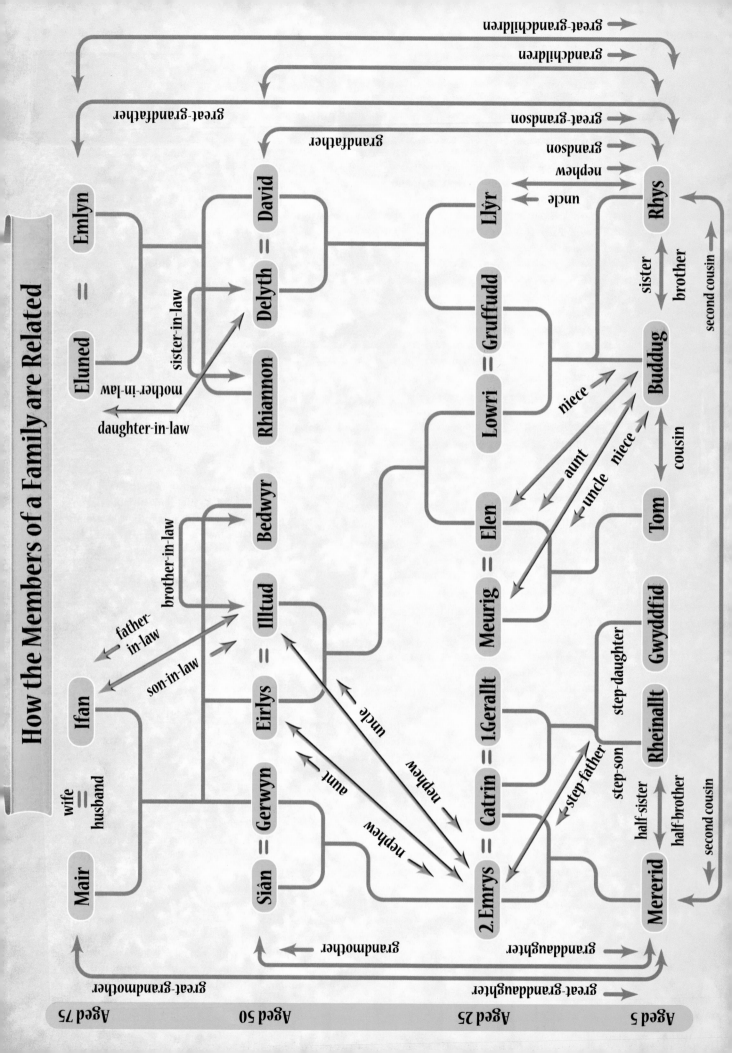

The Princes and Us

It's strange to think that your ancestors were around at the time of the princes. A member of your family may have heard the voice of Llywelyn II or fought beside Owain Glyndŵr. Someone who looked like you, or laughed like you.

History is all around us, and every family has its share of stories, and interesting anecdotes. But how can you find out about your family and make a family tree?

1. First of all, write down the name of every member of the family who is known to you.

2. For more information, it's a good idea to talk to your oldest relative. Find out what he/she remembers about people and events. You could hear some interesting stories!

3. After you've gathered a few names, try and work out how they're all related, with the help of one of your relatives. This chart will show you how to set out a family tree.

4. If you know the names of some of your relatives, a website such as www.ancestry.co.uk will help you find records of them e.g. census returns.

But be careful . . .

It's important to realise that some people would rather not discuss their families. There may have been a family quarrel, or a divorce, or an illegitimate child (a child born to an unmarried mother; years ago not everyone approved).

Robert ap Morris = **Lowri verch Lewis**
Llanfrothen   **ap Ieuan Dafydd**
?–1576   *Ffestiniog*

Morgan Parry = **?**
(yeoman) *Llanwnda*
1679–1761

John Morgan = **Jane Owen**
(yeoman) *Llanwnda*   ?–1810
?–1765

John Jones = **Mary Humphrey**
(farmer) *Betws Garmon*   1781–1831
1757–1838

Owen Jones = **Jane (Siân) Jones**
(cobbler)   1806–1897
Waunfawr
1802–1884

Robert Owen Jones = **Ellen (Elin) Humphreys**
(shop owner)   (shop manageress)
Waunfawr   ?–1936
1840–1921

John Eryri Jones = **Margaret Jones**
(clothes shop owner)   (shop woman)
Bangor   1880–1946
1886–1970

Alun Eryri Jones = **Hulena Hughes Jones**
(bank manager)   (nurse / housewife)
Rhyl / Bangor   1923–2002
1920–1991

Gordon Alderson Jones = **Cerinwen Eryri Jones**
(book editor)   (nurse)
Aberystwyth   1954–
1953–

*

Steffan Eryri Jones   **Adrian Meilyr Jones**
(software developer)   (musician)
Oxford   *Cardiff*
1982–   1987–

Ceri's family*

Here is an example of a simple family tree. There wasn't room to include the names of brothers and sisters.

5

The Britons

The Britons were living in Britain when the Romans arrived in 43 AD. They spoke a language called Brittonic. The Welsh language is descended from Brittonic. When the Romans left Britain in 383, a number of chiefs of the Britons were left in charge of the country. Padarn Beisrudd (Paternus of the red cloak), the grandfather of Cunedda, was one of them.

The earliest known writing in Welsh is on the Stone of Tywyn in St Cadfan's Church, Tywyn.

The Old North

The Old North was the name given by the Welsh to the lands of the Britons in northern England and southern Scotland. After the Romans left in 383, there were many kingdoms in the region with names like Rheged, Elfed and Manaw Gododdin. Little by little the Saxons and the Irish conquered these lands.

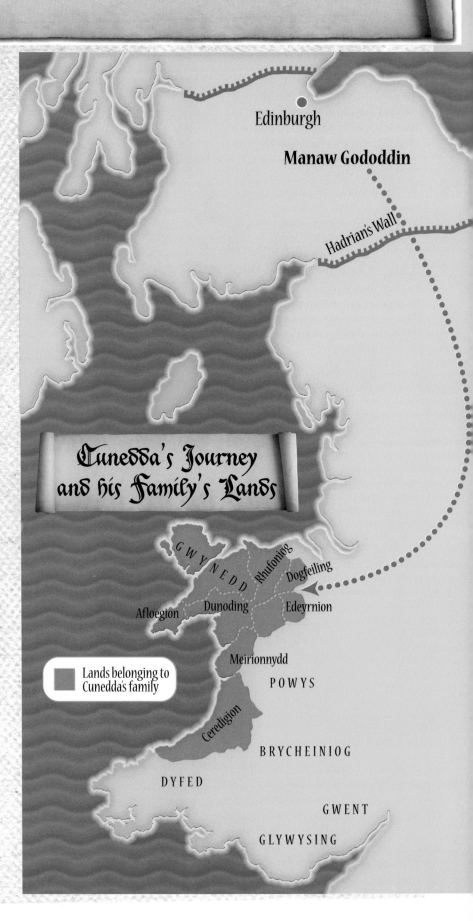

Edinburgh

Manaw Gododdin

Hadrian's Wall

Cunedda's Journey and his Family's Lands

GWYNEDD
Rhufoniog
Dogfeiling
Afloegion
Dunoding
Edeyrnion
Meirionnydd
POWYS
Ceredigion
BRYCHEINIOG
DYFED
GWENT
GLYWYSING

Lands belonging to Cunedda's family

Cunedda Wledig

(sometime between 370–450)

Cunedda was a chieftain of the Old North, who was asked to go to Anglesey to help drive out the Irish invaders. Cunedda took his army, seven of his sons and one of his grandsons to north Wales around the year 380 or 430, and drove the Irish back across the sea. Then Cunedda founded the kingdom of Gwynedd.

Many regions of Wales were apparently named after Cunedda's sons. These include Ceredigion (Ceredig), Edeirnion (Edern), Rhufoniog (Rhufon), Cafflogion in Llŷn (Afloeg). Meirionnydd is named after his grandson, Meirion. Allt Cunedda, near Cydweli, may have been the site of a battle.

Cunedda was known as Cunedda Wledig, with 'Wledig' meaning Lord, prince, or ruler.

Why was Cunedda important?

♛ Cunedda founded the kingdom of Gwynedd. As we shall see, many important princes of Wales came from Gwynedd.

A message for Cunedda, 430

Cunedda was sitting in his court in Manaw Gododdin in the Old North. It was a fine, calm morning in the year 430, with the mist beginning to lift from the valley below. As he looked out across his lands, Cunedda felt happy and at ease. He was a well-respected chieftain, admired by all the Britons, and his sons and grandsons were also brave warriors. No wonder life felt so good.

The peace was broken by the sudden arrival of a servant.

"A messenger has come to see you, my lord," he announced.

"A messenger? Where has he come from?" asked Cunedda in surprise.

"He says he's travelled from Anglesey," the servant replied.

"Have you given him food and drink?" Cunedda asked.

"Yes, and he gulped it down like a wild beast," said the servant with a smile.

"You'd better invite him in then," said Cunedda.

In came the messenger. He looked exhausted, his woollen clothes were dishevelled and his bare feet were red and sore.

"Greetings to you, my lord," he panted. "I have an important message."

"Tell me what it is at once," ordered Cunedda.

"I was sent here from Anglesey," said the messenger. "For days I sailed aboard ship, then I ran all the way from the coast."

"Why the hurry?" asked Cunedda.

"Anglesey is in danger," said the messenger. "Since the departure of the Romans, the Irish keep crossing the sea and attacking us. They are burning our houses, taking our children slaves and stealing our treasures. There's no stopping these pagans. They have no respect for Christians such as ourselves. Will you come and lead us in battle against them? Without your help, we'll lose all our lands and the pagans will rule us."

Cunedda was astonished. He hadn't expected such a message. Though he had heard rumours of skirmishes in various parts of Britain, he hadn't realised that the situation was so bad. It was so desperate, he had to come to a decision as soon as possible. Cunedda thanked the messenger and told him he would have his answer shortly.

Though Cunedda was happy in the Old North, it took him no time at all to make up his mind. He must lead his family and his army in battle against the Irish.

It was his duty to defend Britain against the pagans.

* * *

Some years later, Cunedda looked out from his court at the mountains of Snowdonia and thought how much had changed since the day that message arrived. He and his sons had journeyed to Anglesey, and after a fierce campaign, had driven back the Irish. Cunedda had then gone on to establish a new kingdom in Snowdonia – the kingdom of Gwynedd. Once again life was good.

Maelgwn Gwynedd

One Country, One King, 520

A white line of foam was now visible out in the bay.

Another line had already formed on the beach – a line of chairs that faced the sea and stretched out along the sand. They were large chairs, carved of the finest oak, each trying to outdo the others in size and height.

Another line had already formed on the beach – a line of chairs that faced the sea and stretched out along the sand. They were large chairs, carved of the finest oak, each trying to outdo the others in size and height.

"The tide has turned!" shouted a voice on the beach.

A tremor of excitement ran through the assembled company. They wouldn't have long to wait.

Some of the men shifted in their chairs. There were many worried faces. Some sat back and instinctively lifted their feet.

The men seated on the chairs had an air of importance. They were dressed in bright costly garments, and one or two wore crowns or heavy chains. Some of the chairs were inlaid with bright, precious metals, and behind each one stood uniformed servants bearing banners.

The banners that fluttered in the wind that whipped the waves weren't ordinary banners – they were coats of arms. The chairs on the beach weren't ordinary chairs – they were thrones. Their bearded, important-looking occupants weren't ordinary men – they were kings.

It was the beginning of the sixth century – around 520 – and this was Aberdyfi beach in mid-Wales. The banks of the Dyfi river had been a convenient meeting-place for the kings and princes of Wales throughout the ages, and these were the men who had gathered on Aberdyfi beach that day.

After the departure of the Romans, many kingdoms were established in Wales, and they were always quarrelling with each other. But there were even more dangerous enemies on the horizon – the pagan hordes who attacked and stole large areas of land. For that reason it was decided that there must be one person to lead all the kings of Wales – a high king whom all the rest must obey.

The kings of every region of Wales were summoned to Aberdyfi to pit their strength against the might of the sea. The challenge was to remain seated as the tide came in and the waves lapped higher and higher. The last to leave his chair and flee inland would be High King of Wales.

The water had already begun to lap around the feet of the seated kings. The servants decided to retreat, taking the banners with them, while their masters anxiously watched as the water rose around their heavy chairs.

But one king had a smile on his face. The chair that his servants had carried to the beach was very different from the others. When his fellow-kings saw it, they sneered. It was a throne made of white feathers glued with wax. A white, untidy throne that, in their opinion, was quite unsuitable for a king.

But as the tide rose around the necks of the other kings, they soon realised the advantage of the untidy throne. It could float on the surface of the sea. While they got wet, the owner of the throne – the cunning Maelgwn Gwynedd – had barely a drop of water on his clothes.

One by one the other kings had to abandon their fine thrones and flee for their lives. Maelgwn Gwynedd, of the court of Deganwy, was proclaimed High King of the Welsh – the king who had won a battle with the aid of a sack of feathers!

The view from Deganwy castle

Why was Maelgwn Gwynedd important?

♛ He became chief king of Wales in the sixth century. As a result, the concept of Wales as a single country became important for the first time.

Maelgwn Gwynedd

(490–549)

Maelgwn Gwynedd was the great-grandson of Cunedda (pp. 6-7). Maelgwn went to school in Llancarfan or Llantwit Major (in Glamorgan) with the aim of being a monk - he was at the school at the same time as Saint Deiniol. However Maelgwn changed his mind and decided to be a king instead. His uncle was on the throne, but that didn't stop Maelgwn. He deposed his uncle and became king in his place. He also defeated the other kings of Wales and became known as dragon, or chief king.

Maelgwn's Court may have been at Dinarth, near Deganwy (Caernarfon). He was said to have been very generous towards the Church. He gave Cybi the site of the Roman fort on which to build a church, and gave land to Deiniol on which to found Bangor church. He was a very tall man, who was also known as Maelgwn Hir (Long Maelgwn). He apparently died of the Yellow Plague. According to legend, he saw the Yellow Plague peeping at him through the church keyhole and shortly after fell down dead.

Above Aberdyfi

Cadwallon ap Cadfan

The battle of Hatfield Chase, 633

The sun was beginning to set, and Cadwallon could see that his soldiers were tired. Some looked exhausted, and no wonder. They had been marching steadily since daybreak, so it was high time they rested for the night. He ordered everyone to stop and set up camp. The soldiers dropped their weapons and heaved a sigh of relief.

Cadwallon himself felt he could have marched all night. Ever since he'd lost a fierce battle at Rhos, near Eglwys-bach, and seen Gwynedd fall into the hands of Edwin, king of Northumbria, Cadwallon had been itching for revenge. After the battle he'd had to escape to Ireland, and for seven long years he'd been plotting to regain Gwynedd. Now it was the year 633, and after winning battles in Gwent and Carmarthen, Cadwallon was ready to face Edwin once more.

But he wouldn't be alone. Penda, king of the English kingdom of Mercia, had agreed to fight with him, since Edwin had stolen parts of his land too. The more soldiers the better, thought Cadwallon bitterly. He couldn't afford to be beaten again by Edwin. He must defeat Northumbria once and for all.

No-one slept well that night. They all knew they were within a stone's throw of the battlefield at Hatfield Chase, just north of Doncaster. They tossed and turned till a glimmer of sun appeared in the east. Then they rose quietly, formed rows, and prepared to face Edwin's army.

The battlefield was very boggy, and nearby the river Don was in full flood. I hope we don't sink into this marsh, thought Cadwallon. No, we won't, he told himself. We must be strong and determined. Still, it was natural to feel on edge. The next few hours would be crucial.

Edwin and his sons Osfrith and Eadfrith appeared at the head of a large Northumbrian army. Cadwallon and Penda looked at each other. The time had come at last.

"To battle!" roared Cadwallon, and his army rushed forward to meet the enemy. Noises rent the air: the clash of sword against shield, yells of excitement, the unearthly screams of soldiers ripped apart by spears, and the sound of dead bodies falling on the boggy ground. The air was filled with the stench of battle – the stench of mud, sweat and blood.

It was all over long before sunset. Now the only sound was the excited croak of the ravens as they fluttered from corpse to corpse. It was a good day for the ravens, who had plenty of bodies to feed on. But it was a disaster – for the men of Northumbria. Edwin and Osfrith lay dead, and Eadfrith had been captured by Penda.

Cadwallon was overjoyed; he had taken his revenge on Edwin, and had regained Gwynedd at last. He would now lay waste to the kingdom of Northumbria and make sure that it could never again threaten Gwynedd.

Cadwallon ap Cadfan

(600–633)

Cadwallon was a descendant of Maelgwn Gwynedd. At this time kings from outside Wales were trying to attack Gwynedd and other Welsh kingdoms. Cadwallon lost an important battle to Edwin, King of Northumbria, near Eglwys-bach in 625, and Edwin became king of Gwynedd. Cadwallon had to flee to Ireland. The story tells of Cadwallon's return to fight Edwin at the Battle of Meigen (Hatfield Chase). He was helped by Penda, king of Mercia. The poem in praise of Cadwallon, written after this victory, contains the word 'Cymry' ('the Welsh'), and may be the first poem ever to do so. After the Battle of Meigen, Cadwallon fought more battles in Northumbria, before being killed in battle at Heavenfield, by Oswald, king of Bernicia. Oswald himself was killed in Oswestry in 634.

Why was Cadwallon ap Cadfan important?

♛ Cadwallon defended Wales from attack in the seventh century

The Kingdoms of the Britons

GWYNEDD	British Kingdom
MERCIA	English Kingdom
⚔	Battle

Dun Breatann (Dumbarton)
Din Eidyn (Edinburgh)
GODODDIN
Lindisfarne
STRATHCLYDE
Bamburgh
BERNICIA
RHEGED
Carlisle
Penrith
Catraeth (Catterick) ⚔
NORTHUMBRIA
DEIRA
York
ELFED
Deganwy
Bangor ⚔ Rhos
Chester ⚔
Hatfield Chase (Meigen) ⚔
LINDSEY
GWYNEDD
Oswestry
MERCIA
EAST ANGLIA
Aberdyfi
CEREDIGION
POWYS
BRYCHEINIOG
DYFED
GLYWYSING
ERGING
Gloucester
ESSEX
GWENT
London
Llancarfan
Bath
KENT
WESSEX
SUSSEX
DUMNONIA
CORNWALL

After William Rees, 1959 and John Davies, 1990

Building Offa's Dyke

Around 780

One morning towards the end of the eighth century, Dafydd Goch stepped out of his wooden house in Powys and had the shock of his life. In the distance a large band of men was making its way towards him.

"What on earth …?" he gasped. "I hope they're not soldiers from Mercia."

Dafydd lived on the border between Powys and the English kingdom of Mercia, so he was always on his guard. Powys and Mercia were always fighting, and he was afraid that the men of Mercia would come over the border one day, and burn his house to the ground. As he watched, the soldiers came to a halt and stood in a long line.

"God help us!" thought Dafydd. "They're going to attack!"

He was about to run into the house to warn his wife, when he saw the men lean forward. Each of them had a spade in his hand. Before his very eyes they began to dig a ditch, throwing each spadeful of soil to the right.

"What's going on?" muttered Dafydd. Already, huge heaps of soil were springing up along the edge of the ditch. Once the heaps had joined up in a long line, Dafydd realised what was happening. He ran into the house, and shouted excitedly to Mali, his wife. "It's a dyke, Mali! The men of Mercia are building a dyke!"

"Building a dyke?" said Mali in astonishment. "What on earth for?"

"Well," replied Dafydd, "I've heard that Offa, king of Mercia, is fed up of being attacked by the men of Powys and Gwent. I expect this is how he's going to defend his border."

"It'll be good for us too," said Mali. "The dyke will show exactly where the border is, so the men of Mercia won't be able to sneak into Powys and steal our lands either."

"That's true," said Dafydd.

For the next days and weeks there was plenty of activity all along the dyke. As the men worked, the ditch got deeper and the dyke grew taller. Dafydd was told that it stretched from the sea in North Wales to the sea in South Wales, and that there were wooden towers here and there where the men of Mercia kept watch. He also heard that they cut off the ears of any Welshman who ventured over the dyke. So Dafydd Goch decided he'd better not try it – and stayed close to home!

Offa's Dyke Centre, Trefyclo

Offa's Dyke
End of the eighth century

Offa, king of Mercia (757–96), decided to build a dyke to protect his kingdom from attack by Powys and other Welsh kingdoms, and also to control movement between Mercia and Wales. This was an enormous undertaking – the dyke stretched for 226 km. Every man in Mercia had to do some work for the king each year, and that was how the dyke was built. There may have been a wooden fence in places, which has rotted away, and that is why there are some gaps in the dyke. It is said that the men of Mercia cut off the ears of any Welshman who ventured over the dyke, and that everyone who came over from Mercia to Wales was hanged.

Today you can walk along Offa's Dyke Path and visit the Offa's Dyke Centre at Knighton in Powys, on the Shropshire border.

Why was Offa's Dyke important?
♛ After the building of Offa's Dyke, there was a well-defined boundary between Wales and England. That was one of the reasons why the two countries developed in different ways.

The Early Kingdoms 400–800

⬭ Offa's Dyke

Offa's Dyke near Presteigne

MÔN (ANGLESEY)

GWYNEDD

RHOS

TEGEINGL (ENGLEFIELD)

RHUFONIOG

● Chester

PENLLYN

EDEIRNION

MEIRIONNYDD

POWYS

MERCIA

ARWYSTLI

Gwrtheyrion

Maelienydd

CEREDIGION

SEISYLLWG

Knighton

ELFAEL

BUELLT (BUILTH)

DEHEUBARTH

YSTRAD TYWI

BRYCHEINIOG

EWIAS

ERGING (ARCHENFIELD)

DYFED

GWENT

MORGANNWG (GLAMORGAN)

GŴYR (GOWER)

GLYWYSING

After William Rees, 1959 and John Davies, 1990

Rhodri Mawr (Rhodri the Great)

Celebrating Rhodri's Success, 871

One late afternoon in 871 there was great activity at Rhodri Mawr's court in Gwynedd. The menservants were moving the benches in the great hall, and the maids were laying the tables. One man was throwing logs onto the open fire in the centre of the hall, and a long column of smoke rose towards the hole in the roof. Wafts of the most delicious smells floated in from the kitchen.

Soon the hall began to fill. First came the noblemen who took their places on the benches beside the long tables. Next came the retinue, the king's household who included soldiers and court officials. Among them were Rhodri's six sons. Then came the chief officials of the court: the Head of the Household, the Priest, the Chief Steward, and the Justice. They all sat at the high table, each side of the king's wooden throne and his wife Angharad's special chair.

The noblemen, the important members of Rhodri's kingdom, were buzzing with excitement and talking nineteen to the dozen. Why had Rhodri invited them all to his court? There was rumour of an important announcement. In front of them the tables were already laden with delicious foods and plenty of mead and ale. The king's retinue and the chief officials looked very pleased. They obviously knew what Rhodri was about to say.

The Chief Steward stood up, called for silence and asked everyone to rise. Rhodri and Angharad walked into the hall and stood at the table. After the Priest had offered a short prayer, Rhodri began to speak:

"Welcome to you all to this very special feast. I'm very pleased to see you. As you know, we managed to unite the kingdoms of Gwynedd and Powys some fifteen years ago. Now I have excellent news. The day before yesterday, our soldiers fought against the men of Seisyllwg. If you haven't already heard, I'm pleased to announce that we won that battle, and captured the lands of Seisyllwg. So it gives me great pleasure to announce that the kingdoms of Gwynedd, Powys and Seisyllwg are one. Our rule now extends over the greater part of Wales!"

Everyone began to shout and applaud. "Long live King Rhodri! Long live Rhodri Mawr!"

There was great celebration in Rhodri's court that night. After the feasting was over, the storyteller came to tell his tales, and the bards recited poems in praise of Rhodri's bravery in battle and his generosity at court. The entertainment lasted for hours and the guests had the time of their lives. No-one enjoyed himself more than Rhodri Mawr. After all, he now ruled almost the whole of Wales.

A Feast in the Court of Rhodri

Poet · Priest · Head of Household · Rhodri · Angharad · Justice · Steward · Rhodri's sons · Musician · Commoner · Soldier

Rhodri Mawr

(820–878)

Rhodri became king of Gwynedd in 844, on the death of his father, Merfyn Frych. He became king of Powys in 856 and king of Seisyllwg around 871. His wife, Angharad, belonged to the royal family of Seisyllwg.

He was kept busy fighting the English of Mercia who attacked Powys, and the Vikings, who attacked from the sea. He won a great victory in 856, when he killed Horm the Northman near the Little Orme, Llandudno.

Maybe that was why he was called 'Mawr' ('Great'). In England, Scotland and Ireland, the Northmen killed many kings, and captured a lot of territory. But because of Rhodri's bravery, they failed to do so in Wales. Although there are Norse names in Wales, e.g. the islands of Skomer and Skokholm, the Vikings were unable to settle in the country.

Rhodri Mawr was killed in battle against the English of

Mercia in 878, as was Gwriad, one of his sons. Later, Anarawd, another of his sons, managed to defeat the English in a battle known as 'Rhodri's Revenge' near Conwy. It was Anarawd who inherited Gwynedd and Powys. His brother Cadell inherited the kingdom of Seisyllwg.

Bardsey island

Why is Rhodri Mawr important?

Rhodri is one of two Welsh king who were called 'Mawr' ('Great'). He made two very important contributions:
- ♛ He united the three most important Welsh kingdoms: Gwynedd, Powys and Deheubarth.
- ♛ He defended his country against the English and the Vikings.

Ramsey island

Who were the Vikings?

The Vikings (or Northmen) came from northern Europe (the present-day countries of Norway, Denmark, Sweden and Finland). They were pagans, and began to attack the coast of Wales in the ninth century.

The existence of Norse place names is proof of their presence in certain areas of Wales: Swansea, from Sveinn (a man's name) + ey (an island). The name Anglesey comes from Ongull (a man's name) + ey (an island). The names of the islands of Skomer, Bardsey and Caldey also come from the Norse.

Hywel Dda

A law for the whole of Wales, around 943

"Did you remember to bring a copy of our laws?" Rhys ap Bedwyr asked his friend, Tudur ab Owain. It was during Lent, a few weeks before Easter, and the two noblemen from Cantref Mawr were on horseback. They had just left Carmarthen on their way to Whitland

"Yes, yes, don't you worry," replied Tudur. "I've remembered to bring our laws. And I re-read Hywel Dda's invitation before leaving Manordeilo this morning. I've got it here in my pocket." Tudur pulled out a piece of parchment and showed it to Rhys.

'A special assembly in Whitland, during Lent, 943, to put the laws of Wales in order. Representatives required from every cantref. Bring your laws with you. Hywel ap Cadell of Dinefwr.'

"There'll be a lot of churchmen present, so I've heard," said Rhys, "They want to make sure that the laws follow the teachings of the Bible."

"Of course they do," said Tudur. "I hope all goes well. I've heard that the men of Gwynedd aren't too keen on Hywel's plan. They're afraid that we in Deheubarth have adopted too many Irish practices. They won't accept them, so they say."

"I'm not too worried," said Rhys. "I'm sure the best justices of Hywel's court will be present. They'll make certain that only the best laws are included."

"Have you seen the new coins?" asked Tudur, as they approached Whitland. "I've got one here. Look, it's got an inscription – HOVAEL REX.

That means King Hywel in Latin.'

"That's the first one I've seen," said Rhys. "I think it's excellent. Paying with coins will be much easier than paying with cattle, won't it?"

"Yes," agreed Tudur. "Look over there. Can you see all those people in the field? That must be where the assembly's taking place."

"You're right," said Rhys. "They're about to sit down in a circle around Hywel. Hurry up. I think we're a bit late."

The two men spurred their horses, and galloped towards the assembly.

* * *

A few weeks later, the two - noblemen were riding home.

"That was an excellent assembly," said Rhys. "It was long, but it was worth it."

"It certainly was," said Tudur. "Wales has laws that we can all

be proud of. We forgive people instead of punishing them, and we make wrongdoers pay compensation instead of taking revenge on them."

"Which were your favourite laws?" asked Rhys.

"Well," replied Tudur, "I'm glad that people won't be punished for stealing the food they need to keep themselves alive. In England, the poor are hanged for taking food, but we will forgive them. And I like the fact that every child has the same rights before the law."

"The women of Wales will be treated fairly too," said Rhys. "They'll be allowed to own property, even after marriage. That doesn't happen in England. Over there only men are allowed to own property."

"Yes, I know," said Tudur. "And our laws place a special emphasis on the family. If one member of the family is a murderer, everyone in the family has to pay compensation."

"That's the payment known as 'galanas', isn't it?" said Rhys.

"That's right," said Tudur. "Everyone in Wales will have to make sure they know who their relations are, up to the ninth generation (fifth cousin), in case they have to pay compensation one day."

"Everyone at court now knows exactly what his job involves too," said Rhys. "From the Priest to the Cook, and from the Judge to the Blacksmith."

"All in all, I think Hywel Dda has put our laws in excellent order," said Tudur.

"Yes, he has," said Rhys, "and I'm sure that everyone in Wales will agree."

hywel DDA
CANOLFAN CENTRE

Hywel Dda (Hywel the Good)
Around 850–950

A picture of Hywel Dda in Peniaerth 28 manuscript

Hywel Dda was the grandson of Rhodri Mawr (pp. 14-15) and the son of Cadell. He reigned between the years 910 and 950. After ruling Ceredigion, Ystrad Tywi and Gower, he married Elen, daughter of the king of Dyfed, which then brought all the kingdoms of Deheubarth under his control. As the years went by, he also became prince of Gwynedd, Powys and Brycheiniog.

Hywel is the only prince of Wales to be called 'Good', probably as a result of travelling to Rome to visit the Pope. He is also the only one to have coins bearing his name.

The age of Hywel was very peaceful. He tried to keep the peace by avoiding any confrontation with the kings of England. Every year he paid tribute (20 pounds of gold, 300 pounds of silver and 25,000 oxen) to Athelstan, king of England.

The meeting to consolidate the laws of Wales, which Hywel arranged in the 940s, is today commemorated in his Memorial Garden in Whitland. In the garden, designed by Peter Lord, many of the laws are on display.

Siambr Hywel (Hywel's Chamber) is the name of the debating chamber for children and young people in the Assembly buildings in Cardiff Bay. Children from all over Wales can go there to discuss matters of importance to them, and to vote on them. The name is very appropriate, because children were given a special mention in the laws of Hywel Dda. Wales was also the first country to appoint a Children's Commissioner.

Today women play an important role in the Welsh National Assembly, just as they did in the laws of Hywel Dda. Half the members of the Assembly are women. In the Westminster parliament in London only 25 per cent of the members are women.

The laws of Hywel Dda no doubt influenced the Welsh settlers who went to Patagonia at the end of the nineteenth and the beginning of the twentieth century, because they were the first to give women the vote.

Extract from the Latin text of Hywel's laws

'Siambr Hywel' in the Assembly building

Hywel Dda Memorial Garden, Whitland

Why was Hywel Dda important?

Hywel's special contribution was:
- ♛ to gather together the various legal traditions of Wales and put them in order, so that there was one law for the whole of Wales
- ♛ to make sure that the laws were fair and civilised – to forgive was better than to punish
- ♛ to rule over every part of Wales except Glamorgan and Gwent
- ♛ to keep Wales at peace by recognising the authority of some of the English kings.
- ♛ In Wales, by the end of Hywel's reign, there was one language (Welsh), one religion (Christianity) and one law (the laws of Hywel Dda).

Land in Hywel Dda's time
Hundred/Cantref and Commote

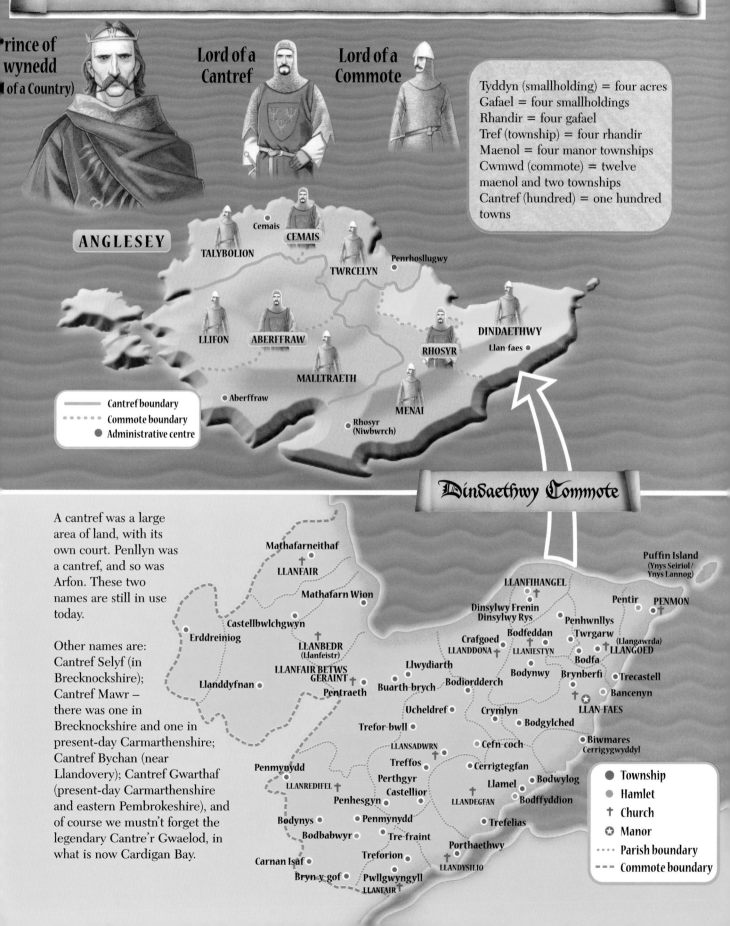

Prince of Gwynedd (Lord of a Country)

Lord of a Cantref

Lord of a Commote

Tyddyn (smallholding) = four acres
Gafael = four smallholdings
Rhandir = four gafael
Tref (township) = four rhandir
Maenol = four manor townships
Cwmwd (commote) = twelve maenol and two townships
Cantref (hundred) = one hundred towns

ANGLESEY

Cemais · **CEMAIS**
TALYBOLION
TWRCELYN
Penrhosllugwy
LLIFON   **ABERFFRAW**
DINDAETHWY
RHOSYR   Llan-faes ·
MALLTRAETH
MENAI

— Cantref boundary
···· Commote boundary
· Administrative centre

· Aberffraw
· Rhosyr (Niwbwrch)

Dindaethwy Commote

A cantref was a large area of land, with its own court. Penllyn was a cantref, and so was Arfon. These two names are still in use today.

Other names are: Cantref Selyf (in Brecknockshire); Cantref Mawr — there was one in Brecknockshire and one in present-day Carmarthenshire; Cantref Bychan (near Llandovery); Cantref Gwarthaf (present-day Carmarthenshire and eastern Pembrokeshire), and of course we mustn't forget the legendary Cantre'r Gwaelod, in what is now Cardigan Bay.

Mathafarneithaf
LLANFAIR
Mathafarn Wion
Castellbwlchgwyn
Erddreiniog
LLANBEDR (Llanfeistr)
Llanddyfnan
LLANFAIR BETWS GERAINT
Pentraeth
Buarth-brych
Llwydiarth
Bodiordderch
Ucheldref
Trefor-bwll
LLANSADWRN
Penmynydd
Treffos
LLANREDIFEL
Perthgyr
Castellior
Penhesgyn
Bodynys
Penmynydd
Bodbabwyr
Tre-fraint
Carnan Isaf
Treforion
Bryn-y-gof
Pwllgwyngyll
LLANFAIR

Puffin Island (Ynys Seiriol / Ynys Lannog)
LLANFIHANGEL
Pentir   PENMON
Dinsylwy Frenin
Dinsylwy Rys
Penhwnllys
Crafgoed
Bodfeddan
Twrgarw
(Llangawrda)
LLANDDONA
LLANIESTYN
LLANGOED
Bodfa
Bodynwy
Brynberfi
Trecastell
Bancenyn
LLAN-FAES
Crymlyn
Bodgylched
Cefn-coch
Biwmares
Cerrigygwyddyl
Cerrigtegfan
Llamel
Bodwylog
LLANDEGFAN
Bodffyddion
Trefelias
Porthaethwy
LLANDYSILIO

Legend:
● Township
○ Hamlet
† Church
✪ Manor
···· Parish boundary
--- Commote boundary

Gruffudd ap Llywelyn

A lump of meat in a pot of stew, around 1025

"Gruffudd, where are you?" Gruffudd's sister had been searching for him high and low.

"In the great hall, by the fire," called Gruffudd. "It's nice and warm here."

"Lazing around as usual," said his sister. "Father's going hunting. Why don't you go with him, and learn how to hunt?"

"No thanks," said Gruffudd. "I like lying here watching the flames. It's cold outside, and I don't want to move, thank you very much."

"Lazybones!" snapped his sister. "It's time you realised just exactly who you are – Gruffudd ap Llywelyn, son of Llywelyn ap Seisyll, prince of Deheubarth. You shouldn't be so lazy and cowardly. It's time you were more adventurous, and brave and bold. You'll be a prince one day, remember."

"One day," replied Gruffudd. "But not today." He reached towards the fire and rubbed his hands.

"Why don't you go out tomorrow night?" said his sister. "Perhaps you'll see a sign that will change your life."

"Tomorrow night?" said Gruffudd. "What's so special about tomorrow night?"

"It's New Year's Eve, and everyone will be looking for signs that could change their lives. Don't you remember what happened to Madog ab Ioan last year? He saw two white stones shining in the moonlight, and now he's married to Elen daughter of Dyfrig."

"Best of luck to them both," sniffed Gruffudd. "I don't believe in those old superstitions anyway."

But on the following night Gruffudd did decide to go out. Maybe those old superstitions were true after all. He rode on horseback to the home of one of his friends, and went into the kitchen where the cook was making stew in a huge pot.

"There's something strange happening in this pot," grumbled the cook in a while. "One lump of meat keeps on floating to the top of the pot. Whenever I push it down, it pops up again."

His words struck Gruffudd like a thunderbolt. This was the sign that would change his life!

He was that lump of meat. Although everyone kept knocking him down and criticising him, just like his sister, he was the one who'd end up on top. No-one would be able to keep him down.

From that day on, everyone noticed the change in Gruffudd. He had a strange and determined glint in his eye. If he decided on a course of action, he'd let nothing stand in his way. He would follow his father and become a brave, bold prince.

Gruffudd ap Llywelyn

A Meeting on the banks of the Severn, around 1050

Many years after that New Year's Eve when he saw a sign that would change his life, Prince Gruffudd ap Llywelyn stood on the banks of the river Severn. He was a man of striking appearance: tall, strong and handsome. Gathered around him was a large company of soldiers and noblemen, but there was no doubt that Gruffudd was their leader. He was wearing his finest clothes and on his head was a shining crown.

Gruffudd was now prince over the whole of Wales. He had become prince after his father Llywelyn was killed in 1023. He had won battles against the Vikings on the coast, against the English who tried to cross Offa's Dyke, and against the Welsh

princes of Deheubarth.

On the far side of the river stood Edward the Confessor, king of England, and his retinue. Edward and Gruffudd had agreed to meet to arrange a peace treaty. The river Severn marked the boundary between Wales and England, so it was a good place to meet. Still, neither man wanted to leave his own land; they were far too proud.

For a long time they eyed each other. They were almost the same age, and both equally determined. It didn't look as if either was willing to give in and cross the river.

Edward knew that Gruffudd was a very determined man; his many victories proved as much. They could be there till

night-time. One of them had to make the first move.

At last, Edward came to a decision. He walked to a boat at the river's edge, stepped in and began to row towards Gruffudd.

When he saw Edward nearing the Welsh bank of the river, Gruffudd jumped into the water to greet him. He dragged the boat to shore and made an extraordinary gesture: he lifted Edward from the boat and carried him on his back to dry land.

So Gruffudd ap Llywelyn showed that although he was a powerful prince, he was ready to submit to an even mightier king.

Gruffudd ap Llywelyn (1007-1063)

- ♛ Son of Llywelyn ap Seisyll, prince of Deheubarth
- ♛ He became prince of Gwynedd and Powys in 1039.
- ♛ He fought fiercely against the English on the border between Powys and Mercia.
- ♛ He managed to bring Powys, Gwynedd and Deheubarth under his control.
- ♛ He had to flee from his court in Rhuddlan to the mountains of Snowdonia, when Harold of Wessex attacked him.
- ♛ He was murdered by a Welshman, and his head was sent to King Edward the Confessor.

Why was Gruffudd ap Llywelyn important?

- ♛ He managed to protect the country from the English and the Vikings for 24 years.
- ♛ He united the whole of Wales before the arrival of the Normans.

Gruffudd ap Cynan

Chester Square, 1093

It's the year 1093, and life hadn't been too good to me, Gruffudd ap Cynan. I've been in Chester prison for twelve years, even though I am prince of Wales!

As I smooth down my fair hair, I try yet again to work out what's gone wrong with my life. Although I'm prince of Wales, I've spent most of my life in prison or in exile in foreign lands.

It's the Normans' fault, I know that for certain. They conquered England in 1066 after the Battle of Hastings, when I was eleven years old. Soon the new king of England, William the Conqueror, gave the March, the lands between Wales and England, to three Norman earls. A shudder goes through me when I think of those Marcher earls. Instead of staying in the March, all three have been trying to steal land from their neighbours in Wales. Once they've invaded a territory, they build castles of mud and wood. By now I'm sure they've built hundreds of these motte and bailey castles.

There's one particular earl whom I despise: the Earl of Chester, Hugh of Avranches, or 'Fat Hugh', as we Welsh call him. He is a cruel, loathsome man. He and his cousin, Robert of Rhuddlan, attacked north Wales and tried to capture Gwynedd. But they were soon sent packing. I set sail with my fleet from Ireland to Porth Clais, near St David's. Then, after defeating Trahaearn, prince of Gwynedd, in battle in Pembrokeshire with the help of Rhys Tewdwr, prince of Deheubarth, I travelled to the north to lay claim to Gwynedd.

Yes, those were the days, back in 1081. But I still hadn't crushed Hugh and Robert. They decided to play a cruel trick on me. One day I had a message from Robert of Rhuddlan. He said he wanted to meet me at Rhug in Edeirnion. He'd had enough of fighting and wanted to discuss peace terms.

I went to that meeting with a band of my best archers. But there weren't enough of them. The meeting was a trick. We were captured by Robert's soldiers. I was taken to Chester prison, and my archers' fingers were cut off, so that they would never again use a bow and arrow.

There we are. There's no point in dwelling on the past. But I'm sick to death of looking out through the narrow window of my cell at the town of Chester. It's market day. The air is reeking of food and animals, and ringing to the sound of buying and selling, But now I hear another noise, the sound of shuffling footsteps coming closer and closer to my cell, and the groans of someone who has difficulty in walking. I know who it is before the door opens. Fat Hugh.

"Come on, Gruffudd ap Cynan, prince of Wales," sneers Hugh. "You're going down to to the town square today. Everyone wants to see you, especially the Welshmen who are selling goods in the market."

And soon, here I am in my rags and my chains, in the town square. And not for the first time either. Fat Hugh is delighted. "Come and see Gruffudd ap Cynan, prince of Wales," he

shouts. "Come and spit on him. The rogue deserves no better." My blood boils, but all I can do is sit meekly on the floor.

Off goes Hugh – to feed his fat stomach, most probably – and leaves me in the care of two tired-looking soldiers. Soon, I notice someone lurking near the town wall. A very tall young man, strong and well built. Slowly he comes closer.

"Prince, don't let anyone see you talking to me," says the young man. "I'm going to free you."

"Who are you?" I whisper.

"Cynwrig Hir from Edeirnion," he replies. "My brother was one of the archers who lost his fingers when you were captured."

I fix my blue eyes on him. "Be careful, Cynwrig," I tell him. "If Fat Hugh sees you, he'll show you no mercy. You'll be hanged immediately."

"Don't worry," whispers

Chester cathedral today

Cynwrig. "I can see gaps in the links on your chains. It won't take me long to pull them apart. But I'll have to spit at you, so the soldiers will think I'm an Englishman."

For the next few minutes Cynwrig works on the chain. I try to keep calm, though my heart is beating like a drum. Because of me this young man from Edeirnion is in mortal danger.

Then I realise that Cynwrig has disappeared. Cautiously, I look around me, taking care not to alert the soldiers. From the corner of my eye, I see Cynwrig lurking by the town wall. Then I look down and, to my astonishment, my chains are in pieces!

My two guards aren't even looking at me. They're talking to each other, with their backs to me. The town has gone quiet, so slowly I get to my feet and move towards Cynwrig. We both make our way very cautiously towards the town gate, past the guards. No-one shouts after us, thank goodness.

After we've gone through the gate, we walk faster and faster, and then start running. I, Gruffudd ap Cynan, Prince of Wales, am free for the first time in twelve years!

Gruffudd ap Cynan

(1055–1137)

Gruffudd ap Cynan was born in Dublin and educated at Swords monastery, near Dublin. He was descended from the royal families of Ireland, Wales and the Vikings, and is described as having fair hair and blue eyes.

His father died when he was young, but his mother Rhagnell never let him forget that he had a claim to the kingdom of Gwynedd. When he was 20 years old, the king of Dublin lent him a ship, so that he could sail to Gwynedd. Trahaearn was prince of Gwynedd at the time. Gruffudd failed in his attempt to defeat Trahaearn, and had to flee back to Ireland. On Gruffudd's next visit to Wales, in 1081, he landed at Porth Clais, near St David's. With the help of Rhys ap Tewdwr (father of Gruffudd, Gwenllïan's husband p. 28 and grandfather of Lord Rhys p. 36), prince of Deheubarth, he defeated Trahaearn in battle at Mynydd Carn, in Pembrokeshire. The story tells of the trick played on Gruffudd by Robert of Rhuddlan, his imprisonment by Fat Hugh of Chester, and his escape in 1093. He then fled to Aberdaron and sailed to Ireland. In 1094 he captured the Norman castle at Nefyn. By 1101, after Fat Hugh's death, Gruffudd was willing to recognise the authority of King Henry I, and was given lands in Gwynedd by the king. Gruffudd ap Cynan ruled Gwynedd for nearly 40 years, until his death in 1137 at the age of 82. He lived an exceptionally long life, in an age when many died very young. Gruffudd ap Cynan was blind at the time of his death. He was buried in Bangor Cathedral.

Why was Gruffudd ap Cynan important?

- ♛ Gruffudd ap Cynan managed to protect Gwynedd from the Normans, when they first arrived in Wales.
- ♛ Gwynedd was very prosperous, when Gruffudd was its prince. He did a lot of excellent work, such as planting forests, gardens and orchards, and building new structures, including great churches.

The Welsh Marches

This was the name of the territory on the border between Wales and England. It formed a sort of corridor between the two countries. After the Normans won the Battle of Hastings in 1066, three Earls were put in charge of the Marches: the Earl of Hereford, the Earl of Shrewsbury, and the Earl of Chester. 'Fat Hugh' was the name given by the Welsh to Hugh of Avranches, Earl of Chester. Soon the earls began to steal land from neighbouring princes.

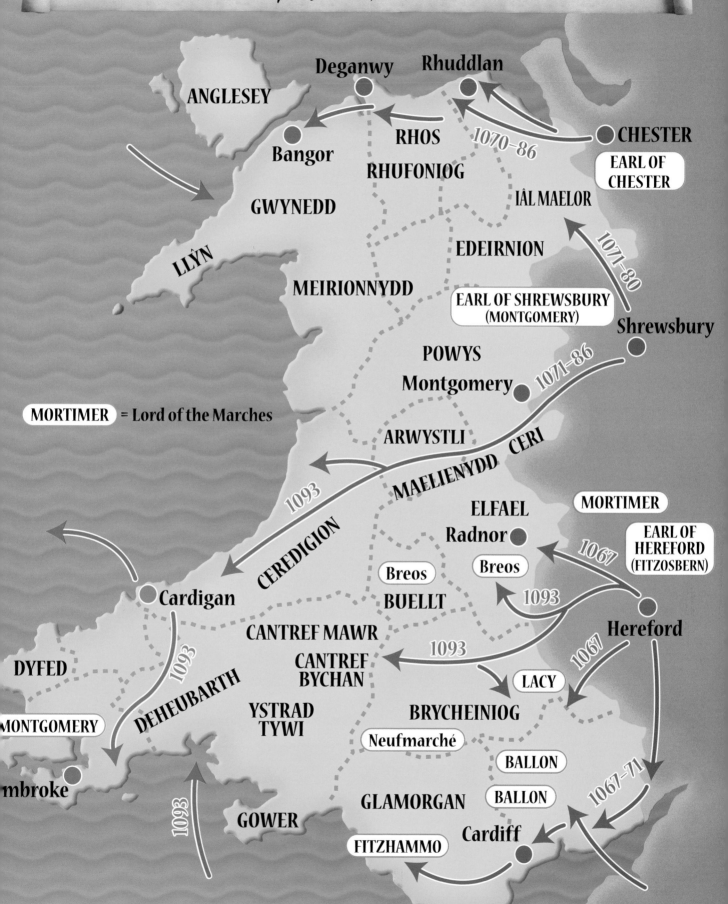

The Main Campaigns of the Normans

Deganwy • **Rhuddlan** •

ANGLESEY

CHESTER •

1070–86

EARL OF CHESTER

RHOS

Bangor •

RHUFONIOG

IÂL MAELOR

GWYNEDD

EDEIRNION

LLŶN

EARL OF SHREWSBURY (MONTGOMERY)

MEIRIONNYDD

1071–80

Shrewsbury •

POWYS

Montgomery •

1071–86

MORTIMER = Lord of the Marches

ARWYSTLI

CERI

MAELIENYDD

1093

MORTIMER

ELFAEL

CEREDIGION

Radnor •

1093

EARL OF HEREFORD (FITZOSBERN)

1067

Breos

Breos

Cardigan •

1093

BUELLT

CANTREF MAWR

1093

DYFED

1093

CANTREF BYCHAN

LACY

Hereford •

1067

DEHEUBARTH

YSTRAD TYWI

BRYCHEINIOG

MONTGOMERY

Neufmarché

BALLON

1067–71

mbroke •

1093

GOWER

GLAMORGAN

BALLON

FITZHAMMO

Cardiff •

After William Rees, 1959; John Davies, 1990, and Hefin Mathias, 1996

Who were the Normans?

The word 'Norman' is very like 'Norseman', another name for the Vikings. The Normans' ancestors were Vikings who had settled in Northern France in the tenth century.

In 1066, the army of William, Duke of Normandy in Northern France, sailed across the Channel to fight Harold, king of England, at Hastings. William's army of 7,000 soldiers defeated Harold's men. The Normans rode horses that had been specially trained. Their soldiers were protected by armour made of strong iron, and helmets of steel. After capturing a territory, they would build castles. To begin with, they built motte and bailey castles, each castle consisting of a wooden structure, set on top of a mound. Later they built stone castles, because the Welsh set fire to the wooden ones. The stone tower of Cardiff Castle can still be seen on its original mound.

Near the castle the Normans set up a borough – a place where more than five people lived. Boroughs were set up throughout Wales. People who lived in boroughs had certain rights.

By 1093 the Marcher Lords (see The Marches p. 24) had captured lands in Gwynedd in the north, Gwent, Glamorgan and Gower in the south, and mid-Wales as far as Cardigan and Pembrokeshire.

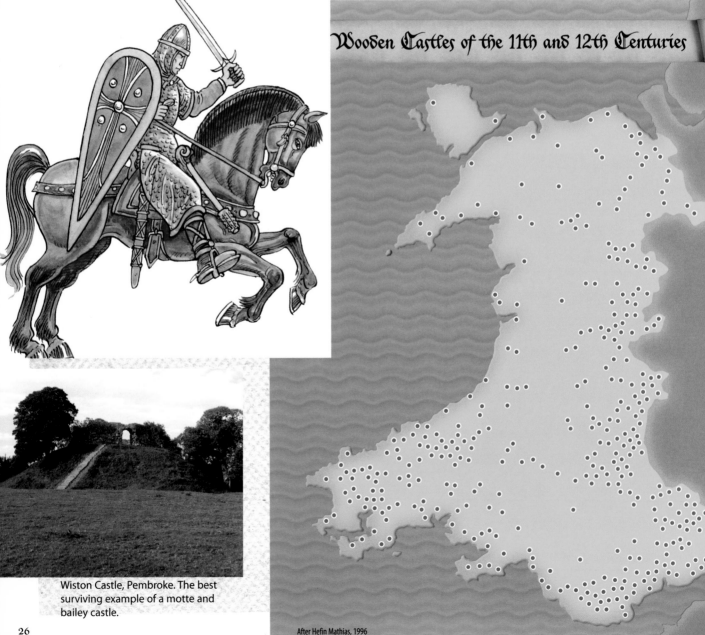

Wiston Castle, Pembroke. The best surviving example of a motte and bailey castle.

Wooden Castles of the 11th and 12th Centuries

After Hefin Mathias, 1996

A Wooden Motte and Bailey Castle

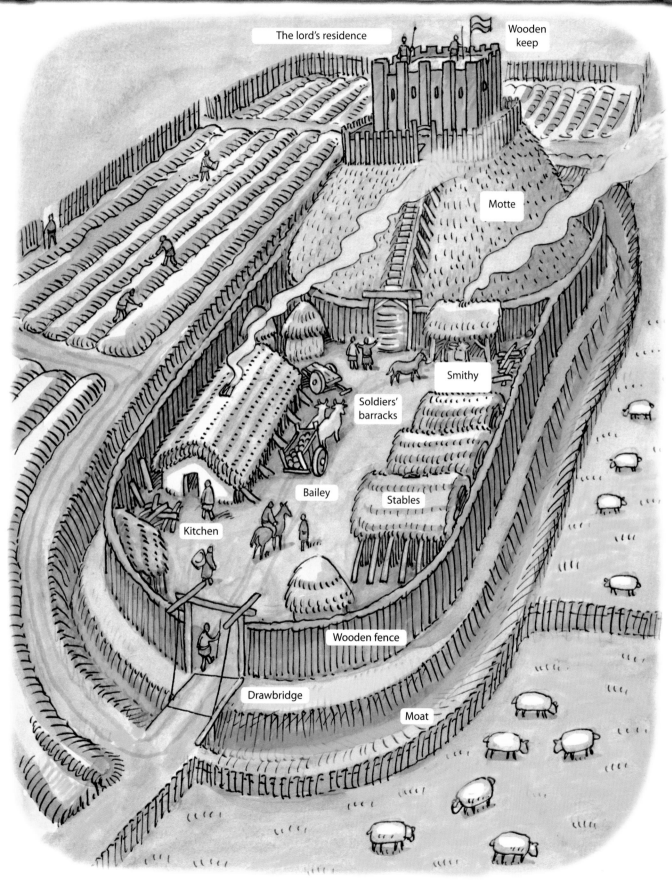

The lord's residence

Wooden keep

Motte

Smithy

Soldiers' barracks

Bailey

Stables

Kitchen

Wooden fence

Drawbridge

Moat

Gwenllïan, daughter of Gruffudd ap Cynan

The heroine of Gwenllïan's Field, 1136

The soldiers of the Welsh army stood with their backs to the river Gwendraeth. On the level field, some were watching the approach of the Norman cavalry from the direction of Cydweli in the south. Others faced east and west, in case of enemy attack from the woods and rocky slopes of Mynydd y Garreg above.

The sun shone on the glistening armour of the Normans; the wind whipped their brightly-coloured banners. The Welsh, for their part, wore leather and cloth. Many carried farm tools instead of weapons.

There was one other great difference between the Welsh army and the Norman forces. The enemy leader was a hard-bitten soldier called Maurice de Londres, but the leader of the Welsh was a woman called Gwenllïan.

Gruffudd ap Rhys, Gwenllïan's husband, had gone to Gwynedd. He wanted to recruit a large army to attack the Norman castles in south Wales, beginning with Cydweli. His own army of five hundred men was far too small to confront Maurice de Londres, lord of Cydweli castle. So he had gone to Aberffraw in Gwynedd to ask for help from the soldiers of Gruffudd ap Cynan, Gwenllïan's father, and her two brothers.

But in the meantime the Norman spies had heard that Gruffudd was on his way north. Maurice was alarmed at the prospect of fighting Gruffudd's large army, so he decided to try and force Gwenllïan to fight without her husband. He sent to England for reinforcements and told them to come at once to Cydweli castle.

Gwenllïan was in Caeo in Carmarthenshire when she heard the news. What should she do? Should she send a messenger to tell her husband to return, or should she lead the small army in an attack on Cydweli castle before the English soldiers arrived?

She addressed her brave men and, in a rousing speech, urged them to defend their land. The men raised their weapons and shouted her name. They were all ready to follow Gwenllïan, because she herself was so brave in battle. Two of her sons were also experienced soldiers: 18 year-old Morgan and Maelgwn, who was 16.

Gwenllïan divided her army in two. She sent one half eastwards to attack the army that was on its way from England. She herself led the other half through the forests of the Tywi valley and along the river Gwendraeth Fach till they came to a sheltered spot below Mynydd y Garreg. There they would set up camp and wait for their other troops to return, before attacking Cydweli.

Little did Gwenllïan know that she was being led into a trap. Facing her were twice as many archers, swordsmen and horsemen. The little army fought long and hard for Wales, for Gwenllïan, but although they killed large numbers of the enemy, they were eventually overwhelmed. Morgan and many Welsh soldiers were killed, and Maelgwn was taken prisoner.

But what of Gwenllïan herself? She fought with all her strength till she too was captured. She was beheaded on the battlefield. To this day the field is known as Gwenllïan's Field.

When he heard of the death of his wife, Gruffudd ap Rhys and their son Anarawd led a a very determined army back from Gwynedd. Gwenllïan's bravery had roused the red dragon from sleep, and this time the Normans were powerless to resist its flames. In the great battle that took place at Crug Mawr to the north of Cardigan, the Welsh soldiers charged at the enemy shouting their heroine's name: "Gwenllïan! Gwenllïan!" The Welsh went on to win many more victories, and kept the Normans on a tight rein in south Wales for the next fifty years.

Why was Gwenllïan important?

- Gwenllïan could fight as well as any man, and was ready to lay down her life in battle.
- She was determined to defend Welsh land against the Normans. For this reason she is a heroine of Welsh history.

Gwenllïan, daughter of Gruffudd ap Cynan

(1097–1136)

Gwenllïan was the daughter of Gruffudd ap Cynan (p. 22), and the sister of Owain Gwynedd (p. 34), Cadwallon and Cadwaladr. She was brought up in Gruffudd's court in Aberffraw, Anglesey. Like her brothers she learnt all the sporting skills – physical training, games, hunting, and how to handle weapons. She was a beautiful young woman, and as she was the daughter of the most important Welsh prince, the sons of other Welsh princes wanted to marry her.

She married Gruffudd ap Rhys. With this marriage the royal families of Gwynedd and Deheubarth were united. They had four sons: Anarawd, Morgan, Maelgwn and Rhys (Lord Rhys p. 36). Gwenllïan would teach her eldest sons how to fight while her husband led his army against the Normans.

Morgan was killed in the battle of Gwenllïan's Field in 1136, and Maelgwn was captured. At the time Rhys, the youngest son, was only four years old. Gruffudd ap Rhys was killed soon after.

Cydweli castle

Ifor Bach, Lord of Senghenydd

A Diary of the Attack on Cardiff Castle, 1158

I've decided that William, Earl of Gloucester, needs to be taught a lesson. He's always stealing my lands in Senghennydd. Those lands are mine according to the laws of Hywel Dda, but William insists on laying claim to them because he's the Norman Earl. So I'm trying to think of a plan that'll help me regain my land.

* * *

The plan has been drawn up. It's a brilliant plan too, if I may say so. Tomorrow night I'll set it in action!

* * *

Last night, after dark, a small band of us went to Cardiff Castle. The castle is a round tower standing on a huge mound of earth. My men were worried about the numbers of soldiers inside – about 120 knights and archers in all. The first thing we did was to place our ladders against the stone walls of the castle. Then we sneaked up without a sound, so as not to alert the soldiers. Once we reached the top of the tower, we searched for William's bedroom. We guessed it would be in the safest place of all, in the middle of the tower, and we were right!

We rushed into his room and gagged William, his wife Hawys and their son Robert. It was tricky getting them down the ladders, but we managed it without alerting the soldiers. The guards must have been sound asleep! Off we raced on horseback to our hiding-place in Senghennydd forest. And that's where we are now. I've told William they'll be set free as long as he gives me back my land, and a bit extra besides. But if he refuses, I've threatened to kill his wife and son. At the moment he's considering my offer, but I don't think we'll have to wait long for his decision.

* * *

We've just set William and his family free. William has signed a document giving all my land back to me, and more besides. My plan has been a great success!

Why was Ifor Bach important?

♛ His story shows us that the Welsh managed to hold on to their lands and to rebel against the Normans in the twelfth century.

Ifor Bach lived in the twelfth century and was Lord of Senghennydd. This region had not fallen completely into the hands of the Normans, but William, Earl of Gloucester, was always stealing Ifor's land. The story of Ifor reclaiming his lands is told by Gerald of Wales (p. 40).

Ifor was married to Nest, the sister of Lord Rhys (p. 36). Llywelyn Bren (p. 60) may have been a grandson of his.

Ysgol Gynradd Ifor Bach is the name of the Welsh-language primary school in Abertridwr today, and Ifor Bach is the name of the Welsh-language club just a sone's throw from Cardiff Castle.

A Norman Stone Castle

The keep

Garderobe/toilet

Bedrooms

The lord's private chapel and apartment

Great hall

Spiral stairs

Tower

Smithy

Soldiers' barracks

The bailey

Cellar and store

Gatehouse

Portcullis

Stables

Well

Curtain wall

Drawbridge

Great moat

Pembroke castle

Raglan castle

Let's Make a Coat of Arms

Every prince had to have a coat of arms, so how about making your own?

A coat of arms was in the shape of shield. The shield was divided up in different ways:

down the middle (party per pale) — in quarters (party per cross) — across the middle (party per fess) — with a jagged line (party per chevron) — diagonally from top left to bottom right (party per band) — with a cross (party per saltire)

Animals, fish and flowers were often used.
e.g. a lion on its hind legs (rampant)

Owain Glyndŵr

Horse

Eagle

Today, every county council has a coat of arms, as do many other institutions. What is the coat of arms of your county?

The old coat of arms of Gwynedd County Council
[The strength of Gwynedd]

The coat of arms of Rhondda Cynon Taff
[Here to help you]

Before starting work on your coat of arms, look for examples in books and on the web. Decide how you're going to divide up your shield, and then decide on the decoration – animal, fish or flower. You could draw them in each section. How about writing your favourite proverb or saying under the coat of arms?

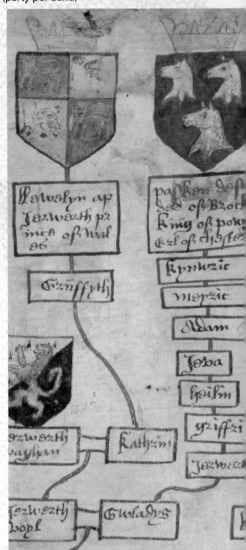

Pedigree roll of Edward Almer of Bantyokyn, Denbighshire, compiled by Rhys Cain in 1602

[Llewelyn ap Iorwerth . . . (Llywelyn the Great)]   [Llowarch ap Brân . . .]   [Riryd Blaith, lord of Penllyn . . .]   [Ednowen Bendew of Tegeingl . . .]   [Pasgen descended of Brochwel, King of Powys . . .]

Welsh Names

Welshmen were named after their father and grandfather. The word 'ap' (or 'ab' before a vowel) means 'son'. Hywel ap Cadell = Hywel son of Cadell; Gruffudd ap Llywelyn ap Rhodri = Gruffudd son of Llywelyn son of Rhodri. (His father's name was Llywelyn, and his grandfather was Rhodri.)
Sometimes an adjective was used to describe a person – Dafydd Fychan = Short Dafydd; Rhys Ddu = Black Rhys/Rhys Goch = Red Rhys (one Rhys had black hair, and the other had red hair), Rhodri Mawr = Rhodri the Great, Hywel Dda = Hywel the Good

The English could not pronounce Welsh names, and so they began to anglicise the names and leave out the 'ap'. As a result, Siôn ap Dafydd became John Davies.

Most Welsh surnames are formed from forenames:
Siôn > Jones
Hywel > Howells
Gruffudd > Griffiths
Ifan > Evans
Dafydd > Davies
Cynrig > Kenrick
Rhys > Rees/Rice

Maredudd > Meredith
Rhydderch > Roderick

The 'ap' or 'ab' can still be seen in these surnames:
ab Ifan > Bevan
ap Hywel > Powell
ap Rhys > Price
ab Owen > Bowen

The adjectives were anglicised too:
Fychan > Vaughan
Goch > Gough
Llwyd > Lloyd / Floyd
Moel > Voyle
Gam > Games
Du > Dee

What is your surname? Do you know of anyone with a Welsh name, such as 'Ieuan ap Huw', or Mari Siôn instead of Mari Jones? How would you make your name sound more Welsh?

Owain Gwynedd and Henry II

A camp on the Berwyn mountains, 1165

"Owain Gwynedd is a thorn in my side," said Henry II, king of England, one afternoon in the spring of 1165. He was furious, and the rings glinted on his fingers as he struck the table before him. "Two years ago he came here to Oxford, and swore an oath of allegiance to me. But what has he been doing ever since? He hasn't been loyal at all. He's been rebelling, and plotting with Louis VII of France to fight against me. That's what he's been doing!"

"You must hit back, sire," said one of his men. "You can't let Owain Gwynedd carry on like this. It's not right. He calls himself 'Prince of Wales', when he writes to the Pope and the king of France."

"I know he does, the rogue," said Henry II. "It's time Owain witnessed the might of England. I'm determined to beat him, whatever the cost."

True to his word Henry II organised a great campaign against the Welsh. The greatest campaign ever. He spent £7,500 – a huge sum at the time – on bringing in extra troops from the continent and from Ireland, and equipping them with the best armour and weapons. His men took cartloads of food, enough to last a few weeks. Then, the huge army gathered at Oswestry. They'd heard that Owain Gwynedd and his supporters had reached Corwen.

"Where's the best place to set up camp?" Henry II asked his advisers. "We'll be meeting the enemy at Glyn Ceiriog."

"The best place is on the Berwyn mountains, sire," one replied. "Owain Gwynedd will be coming from the Corwen direction. If we set up camp on the Berwyn mountains, we'll be within reach of Glyn Ceiriog."

"Excellent," said the king. "The fine summer weather and the mountain breeze will do our soldiers a power of good before the battle."

Confident that they would win an easy victory over Owain Gwynedd, the king and his army set off.

But the king did not realise how high the Berwyn mountains were. Even in August it was cold on the mountaintops. To make matters worse, the weather turned stormy and the army had

to stay put for weeks.

One morning the king was approached by his officers:

"Sire, the cook says our food has run out. The men are weak and starving. They're complaining bitterly. We can't send them into battle in this state."

"What?" Henry was beside himself. "But we've got to fight."

"Our advice is to turn back," said the officers. "There's no point in going on to Glyn Ceiriog. Owain Gwynedd and his soldiers will be far stronger and fitter than we are, after camping down in the valley."

"Coming to the Berwyn mountains was a mistake," said Henry. "A terrible mistake. The whole campaign is a disaster, despite all the money I spent and all the preparations I made. Owain Gwynedd will be laughing at us."

Henry thought long and hard. Then, he smiled slyly.

"Owain may think he's beaten us, but I'll take my revenge on him. Where are the hostages?"

"You mean the Welsh hostages, the children of the Welsh princes, sire? They're here. We meant to hang on to them till after the battle, in case they were needed as a bargaining tool."

"Some of Owain's children are among them, I believe."

"Yes."

"Then beat them harshly and break their arms and legs. And since Owain Gwynedd is still in charge of this miserable little country, they shall never again see the land of Wales. I order you to blind them with hot pokers."

With a satisfied sneer Henry mounted his horse, and headed back towards England.

'Ffordd y Saeson', in the Berwyn mountains

Owain Gwynedd
(reigned from 1137 to 1170)

Owain Gwynedd was the son of Gruffudd ap Cynan (p. 22). He tried to gain land in the north-east, in the direction of Chester, so Henry II, king of England, invaded north Wales. Owain was defeated by Henry in battle near Hawarden, and in 1163, he had to go to Henry's palace at

Woodstock, near Oxford, to swear allegiance to the king.

His nephew, Lord Rhys of Deheubarth (p. 36), and Malcolm, king of Scotland, accompanied him. But Owain Gwynedd and Lord Rhys rebelled against Henry in 1164, so then, as the story tells us, Henry led a great

campaign against Owain during the summer of 1165. Afterwards he decided not to attack Wales again.

Why was Owain Gwynedd important?

- ♛ Owain Gwynedd was the first to call himself Prince of Wales
- ♛ He was the greatest leader of the Welsh in the twelfth century and 'head' of all the Welsh princes of that time.
- ♛ He was followed by other princes, such as Llywelyn ap Iorwerth (p. 46) and Llywelyn ap Gruffudd (p. 51), who wanted to be princes over the whole of Wales.

Castell Carreg Cennen

Lord Rhys ap Gruffudd
The first Eisteddfod, 1176

Celebrating Lord Rhys at the National Eisteddfod

It was Christmas 1175, and Lord Rhys ap Gruffudd of Deheubarth was in his castle in Cardigan. He had captured the castle some ten years earlier, and lately he'd rebuilt it in stone.

He called one of his men to him.

"Do you like this castle?" Lord Rhys asked him, though he knew the answer already.

"Of course I do, Lord Rhys," was the reply. "I'm very proud to live here. You're the first Welsh prince to build a stone castle."

"I am indeed," replied Lord Rhys. "This is my favourite home, although I enjoy staying in Dinefwr every now and then. Listen, I've an idea. I want to show off my castle to everyone. The Great Hall is just the place for a festival. I could invite poets and musicians to come along and compete against each other. What do you think?"

"An excellent idea, sir. What would you like me to do?"

"I want you to let everyone know well in advance. Tell them

the festival will be held in a year's time, at Christmas in 1176. There'll be two competitions …"

"One for poets, and one for musicians?"

"Of course. There'll be a chair for the winner of each competition, and all the noblemen of the kingdom will be invited to a feast."

So, the festival was proclaimed throughout the kingdom, and a year later, the Great Hall of Cardigan castle was full to overflowing.

After everyone had had food and drink, Lord Rhys got to his feet to address the audience. Before him was a splendid sight. All the guests had come in their finest clothes, which were bright and colourful, unlike the grey outfits of the common people. Green and yellow were popular with the men, with a little gold decoration, if they could afford it. The women wore dresses in gold or yellow silk, with a short coat or waistcoat. Some had covered their heads, and wore gold or

jewelled ornaments on their foreheads.

"Thank you for coming to this festival," said Lord Rhys. "I'm very pleased to see you all. I hope you're enjoying yourselves here in Cardigan.

"I must say that I'm far happier today than I was eighteen years ago. If you remember, I was in England at the time, and a prisoner of Henry II. The storyteller will tell you about that period of my life."

The storyteller got to his feet, and began telling the tale:

"Henry planned to attack Dinefwr castle while Lord Rhys was a prisoner in England, so he sent a knight to Wales to gather information. The knight asked a priest called Gwion to take him to Dinefwr along the easiest route. But Gwion was a cunning Welshman, who led the knight along the most dangerous, rocky paths. Every now and then, Gwion would reach down for a handful of grass and eat it. The knight was astonished. He went

back to Henry and told him not to bother with Dinefwr. The paths leading to it were terrible, and the local people were reduced to eating grass like animals! So Henry decided against an attack on Dinefwr, and Lord Rhys was set free!"

Everyone laughed out loud. The guests were thoroughly enjoying the feast and the entertainment. They all had great respect for Lord Rhys, who was generous in peace, and brave as a snarling lion in battle.

Then it was the turn of the poets and musicians. They had come to Cardigan from every corner of Wales. The competitions lasted for hours, and everyone marvelled at the skills of the poets, the harpists, the crwth-players and the pipers. Rhys was very pleased when a harpist from his own court won the musicians' chair. The poets' chair went to a man from Gwynedd, and everyone from Gwynedd cheered loudly.

The feasting and the fun went on for some days, and everyone praised Rhys's festival, the first eisteddfod ever held.

Lord Rhys ap Gruffudd of Deheubarth

(1132–97)

Lord Rhys was the son of Gwenllïan and Gruffudd ap Rhys (p. 28). He was only four years old when his mother was killed near Cydweli castle, and his father was killed soon after.

He led many successful attacks against the Normans, and King Henry II (p. 34) led many campaigns against him.

He was imprisoned for a while in 1163, and then went to pay homage to the king, accompanied by Owain Gwynedd (p. 34). Eventually Henry II became a friend of Lord Rhys, and gave him the post of Justice of South Wales.

Rhys was imprisoned by two of his own sons in 1195. They were quarrelling over who would inherit Rhys's lands after his death. He died in 1197, and was buried in St Davids Cathedral.

The National Eisteddfod was held in Cardigan in 1976, to mark the 800th anniversary of that first eisteddfod.

Why was Lord Rhys important?

- ♛ Lord Rhys was the most powerful of the rulers of Deheubarth. After the death of Owain Gwynedd (p. 34) in 1170, he was the most powerful Welsh ruler.
- ♛ He gave considerable sums of money to the monasteries of Whitland and Strata Florida, and he founded Talyllychau (Talley) abbey.
- ♛ He held the first Eisteddfod in Cardigan in 1176.

Lord Rhys' tomb in St Davids cathedral

Cardigan castle

Dinefwr castle

Welsh Heroes

Statue of Llywelyn the Great, Conwy

The princes were the heroes of their day. Poets praised them in verse, and the Welsh enjoyed hearing tales of their battles and adventures.

Who is your hero or heroine? Here are some Welsh heroes of our time:

Shane Williams
Aaron Ramsey
Dafydd Iwan
Cerys Matthews

Joe Calzaghe

Undefeated

In the Dragon's heart, there burns a steady flame
Determined self-belief is its name,
As a world champion, amongst the greatest ever known
And in his heart there burns a steady flame.
Opponents there were many, as you know
Who tried to get the better of our Joe
But his spirit was too strong, he defeated every one
Opponents there were many, as you know.
Sometimes in life, from nowhere they appear,
Those others who would rule your life through fear,
Get kicks making you feel bad 'cos as characters they're sad,
Sometimes as though from nowhere they appear.
But remember when you'd sooner run and hide,
That Joe and others too, are on your side
Just keep tending to your flame, one day you'll be strong again
It's not your fault you want run and hide,
But the undefeated champ is on your side.

Ray Gravell

I'm Loving Duffy

Can't get enuff-a Duffy
Singing 'bout her pain
Even when I'm in the happiest mood
Especially then.
I'll turn up my iPod
And belt it out with her
Parading my shattered heart,
Leaving no vein unexposed.
I could eat her voice
Like a percussive box of chocolates
Melodic soft centres and deep, dark explosions,
Delicious contrasts melting with soul.
By the time I've arrived at school
I'm satisfied,
I've chomped my way through Rockferry
And I'm invincible.

Both poems by Ruth Morgan

Duffy

Ryan Giggs

These are national heroes – but perhaps you have a local hero or heroine, who is not widely known. Why not write a poem or description of your hero or heroine? See if you can find information about them on the web. You could also add a photograph or a drawing.

Y CYMRO

March 1188

COME AND FIGHT!

Wales is eagerly looking forward to the six-week visit of Archbishop Baldwin of Canterbury. Yesterday the Archbishop commented:

'This is a very special visit. I have come to Wales to try and persuade the Welsh to join the crusade. Last year, Saladin the Turk captured the holy city of Jerusalem, and we must fight to regain it. So, come and take the cross. If you join us, you will be given a red cross to sew on your cloak.'

Archbishop Baldwin hopes to persuade three thousand Welshmen to join the crusade to Jerusalem.

Gerald de Barri, or Gerald the Welshman as we know him, is in the Archbishop's retinue. You may remember that he is related to Lord Rhys, so he can count on a warm welcome in Cardigan. Said Gerald:

'I am looking forward to this visit. I hope to make notes on everything I do and see along the way.'

Graves of princes and abbots at Strata Florida abbey

Gerald the Welshman (Giraldus Cambrensis) (1146–1223)

Gerald was born in Manorbier, Pembrokeshire. His father's family were Normans, and his mother's family was half Welsh. One of his uncles was Bishop of St Davids. He was educated in Gloucester and Paris, then returned to Wales as priest and Archdeacon of Brecon, before spending some years as a teacher of law in Paris.

Gerald travelled widely: in Wales, England and Ireland. He also visited the Pope in Rome on three occasions. He failed to be appointed Bishop of St Davids, probably because his family was partly Welsh. He wrote many books, which are still of interest to us today, such as *The Journey through Wales* and *The Description of Wales*.

Why was Gerald the Welshman important?

♛ Gerald's books have taught us a lot about Wales in the twelfth century

Taith Gerallt Gymro, 1188

During the course of the journey, Gerald wrote a letter to his friend, Stephen de Grey.

Strata Florida Abbey
April 1188

Dear Stephen,

For some weeks I've been travelling through Wales, and I must say I'm enjoying myself. But the important news is that Archbishop Baldwin has persuaded a fair number of Welshmen to take the cross.

Travelling isn't easy: the land is very mountainous or covered in forests. Although there are some Roman roads, the horses often have to travel along footpaths. And strange things have happened! As we crossed the quicksands at the mouth of the river Neath, my horse began to sink! It took several of us to pull him out, otherwise he'd have drowned.

We've had a warm welcome from the Welsh. Sometimes we stay overnight in their simple, thatched dwellings. We lie on reed mats on the earth floors, and share their food. They only eat two meals a day, breakfast and supper. For breakfast they have oat bread and cheese, washed down with a little weak beer or water. In the evening they have stew made of vegetables from their cottage garden. They rarely eat meat. After supper, the Welsh like to chat about their neighbours - who's related to whom, and so on. Everyone knew that my grandmother, Nest, was the daughter of Rhys ap Tewdwr of Deheubarth!

I'm having a wonderful time here in Strata Florida Abbey, and the White Monks are great company. There are about sixty of them in the abbey. It's not easy to get a night's sleep, because the brothers hold eight services throughout the day and night. The first one is at two o'clock in the morning! After the third service at six o'clock in the morning, breakfast is served in the refectory. No one talks during mealtimes, but one of the monks reads from the Bible in Latin. They eat well, and have plenty of bread and wine. Between services the monks copy manuscripts or work in the fields, where they tend the crops or look after the sheep.

As we travel around, the Archbishop addresses the congregations in the new churches that have sprung up in almost every village. They are built of stone, and are in the shape of a cross. They usually have a large door. On the interior walls there are pictures of Bible stories, because the common people can't read the Bible. There are stone benches along the side walls for the use of the noblemen and the elderly, but the common people have to stand in the middle of the church or sit on the reed floor.

I have started to write a book about my journey. Its name will probably be, "The Journey through Wales".

Looking forward to our next meeting.
Yours truly

Gerald de Barri

Gerald's Journey and the Monasteries of Wales

Legend:
- Gerald's Journey — - - -
- Benedictines ✳
- Cistercians ◆
- Franciscans ●
- Dominicans ✚
- Carmelites ▼
- Cluniac ▣
- Augustinians ▢
- Tironians △
- Nunneries †
- Premonstratensian ☐

Locations:
Penmon, Llan-faes, Conwy, Rhuthun, Greenfield, Bangor, St Asaph, Basingwerk, Chester, Caernarfon, Denbigh, Beddgelert, Valle Crucis, Nefyn, Llanfair, Cymer, Strata Marchella, Amwythig, Llanllugan, Tywyn, Cwm-hir, Llanbadarn, Ludlow, Strata Florida, Radnor, Llanllŷr, Llanddewibrefi, Hay, Hereford, Cardigan, Lampeter, St Dogmaels, Talley, Llanthony, St David's, Brecon, Whitland, Abergavenny, Carmarthen, Monmouth, Haverfordwest, St Clears, Usk, Tintern, Pembroke, Cydweli, Llantarnam, Chepstow, Caldey Island, Swansea, Neath, Margam, Basaleg, Caerleon, Newport, Ewenni, Cardiff, Barry Island

A Travel Diary

Gerald kept a diary as he travelled around Wales.

How about keeping your own travel diary, making note of the people and places you see along the way? Unlike Gerald, you could also take photographs. Or how about drawing an occasional picture and colouring it in? Here are some ideas.

An Eisteddfod Diary – the National Eisteddfod or Urdd Eisteddfod in various parts of Wales, or local eisteddfodau. If you compete, write about the competition and the judges. If not, write about the stalls and the evening entertainment.

A Rugby or Football Diary – when you follow your favourite team, write about the game, name the goalscorers. Give each player marks out of ten.

A Swimming Diary – do you compete at weekends? How about writing about your own performance and the performance of the other competitors?

Young Farmers' Club Diary – when you go to a rally, or other competitions, write about your favourite events, about the preparation and the competition itself.

A Rally Diary – maybe you're a fan of rallies and like to watch the cars speeding through the forests of Wales.

A Brass Band Diary – do you travel with the band throughout Wales and England? Describe the competitions and the fun you have amongst yourselves. Who are the most colourful characters?

A Pet Show Diary – do you have an animal or animals that you take to shows? Write about grooming and showing your pet. Describe the other animals in the competition.

43

Monks and Nuns

Many men chose to devote their lives to God, and become monks. They lived in a monastery. Women became nuns, and lived in a nunnery.

In Wales, at the time of Gerald the Welshman, there were different kinds of monks or friars (as shown on the map on p. 42).

Black Monks wore loose black robes. They were Benedictines (Order of St Benedict). The Normans set up many Benedictine monasteries near their castles. The Welsh were not too fond of them, because many came from Normandy.

White Monks wore woollen robes that had not been dyed. They were Cistercians, originally from Cîteaux in France. The Welsh Princes supported them and gave them money.

St Dogmael's abbey

Talyllychau Abbey

The monks spent a lot of time writing. They wrote on parchment, which was animal skin that had been specially prepared for writing and painting. They copied sections of the Bible and recorded the poems of the bards.

Many monks liked to record historical events and did so at the end of each year. The monks of Strata Florida gathered all this information together and compiled a chronicle of Welsh history called *Brut y Tywysogion* (*Chronicle of the Princes*). It gives us an insight into the situation in Wales from the end of the seventh century to the death of Llywelyn II (known as 'Our Last Leader') in 1282.

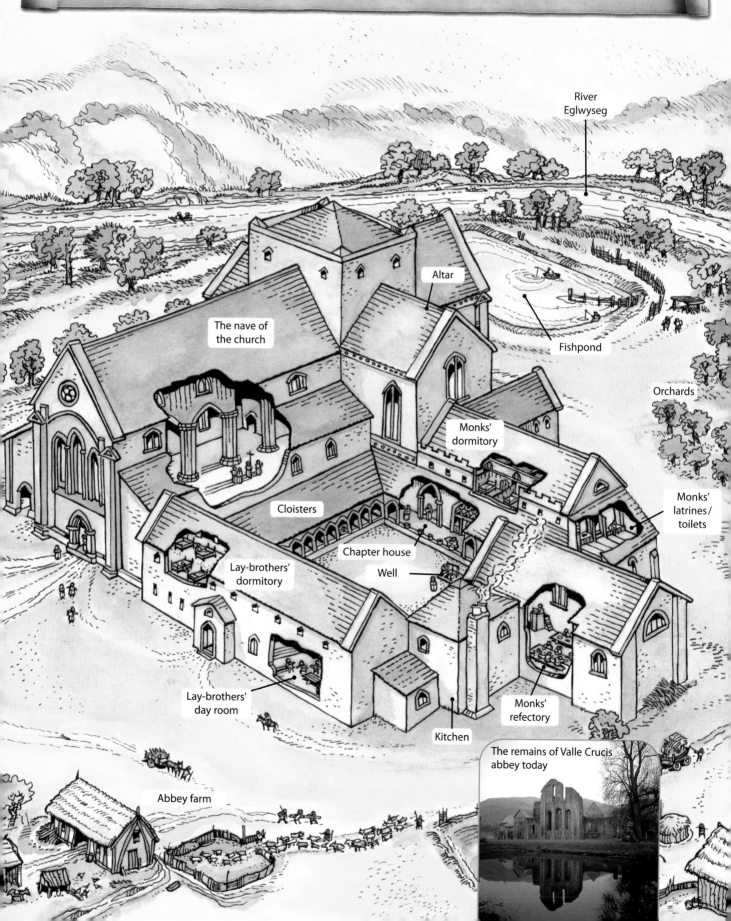

Reconstruction of Valle Crucis Abbey

River Eglwyseg

Altar

The nave of the church

Fishpond

Orchards

Monks' dormitory

Cloisters

Monks' latrines / toilets

Lay-brothers' dormitory

Chapter house

Well

Lay-brothers' day room

Monks' refectory

Kitchen

The remains of Valle Crucis abbey today

Abbey farm

Llywelyn ap Iorwerth (Llywelyn the Great)

A Sunday morning in Trefriw, around 1220

It was a fine Sunday morning in the year 1220, and Llywelyn and his wife Joan were at their court in Trefriw. The prince was standing at his window watching the river Conwy flow past in a blue silken ribbon. He was looking forward to attending the morning service at Llanrhychwyn church, as he did every Sunday.

'I do enjoy the walk up to Llanrhychwyn church,' said Llywelyn. 'It's good to have a breath of fresh air first thing in the morning.'

Joan frowned. Climbing the steep hill to the church didn't appeal to her one bit. She had never dared grumble before, but on this day she spoke out.

'My lord Llywelyn,' she began, 'I know you're very fond of Llanrhychwyn church.'

'Of course I am,' said Llywelyn, putting on a red cloak. 'I was the one who founded the church, less than a mile from here, and very convenient for our Sunday worship.'

'No, it isn't convenient,' said Joan. 'That hill is very steep, and I've had enough of it.'

'What do you want me to do?' snapped Llywelyn. 'Build another church just because you won't climb a little hill?'

'Yes, that is what I want,' said Joan softly. 'Why not build a church here in Trefriw? Then we'd get to church in one minute, instead of in twenty.'

'Joan, Joan!' said Llywelyn. 'You're asking far too much! I've already spent quite enough on building projects - the court in Aberffraw, the castles at Castell y Bere, Cricieth, Dolwyddelan and Dolbadarn, not to mention the money I've given to found monasteries here, there and everywhere. I know you're the daughter of King John of England, and used to having your own way. But I doubt that even he would be willing to build a church just for you!'

'But you should be willing to do so, if only to thank me!' said Joan, raising her voice slightly.

'To thank you? And for what?' asked Llywelyn.

'Have you forgotten that I went to my father?' replied Joan angrily. 'When you two were fighting against each other, I went to him and begged him to make peace. It wasn't easy, believe me. He could well have defeated you, and then you wouldn't be Prince over the whole of Wales. It's all very well forgetting all I've done for you …'

'Joan,' said Llywelyn gently. 'Of course I haven't forgotten all you've done for me. I'm sorry if I sometimes give you that impression.' He looked at his wife with great affection. It was true that he could never have done so well without her. A good wife was a great asset to a prince.

'All right,' said Llywelyn, 'I'll build you a church here in Trefriw … But you'll still have to walk with me to Llanrhychwyn church this morning.'

Llywelyn the Great's coffin in Llanrwst chuch

Llywelyn ap Iorwerth
(Llywelyn the Great) (1173–1240)

Llywelyn ap Iorwerth was the grandson of Owain Gwynedd (p. 34). He had to fight his cousin for the right to be prince of Gwynedd Uwch Conwy. Llywelyn was very ambitious. He wanted to rule over every prince and lord in Wales, and to be Prince of Wales. He married Joan, daughter of King John of England. Llywelyn waged many battles against John, and Joan helped to make peace between them. Llywelyn gave some of his lands in Denbigh to the king, but decided to rebel against him and take back his lands. From 1212 onwards Llywelyn was the most powerful Welsh prince. His title from 1230 onwards was 'Prince of Aberffraw and Lord of Eryri'. Aberffraw was the chief court of Gwynedd and of Wales.

In 1230 Llywelyn caught a man called William de Breos, lord of Brecon and Builth, in his wife's bedroom. William de Breos was hanged at Crogen near Bala before a crowd of around 800 people. Joan was imprisoned for a year, but then returned to live with Llywelyn.

Llywelyn built stone castles at Castell y Bere, Cricieth, Dolwyddelan and Dolbadarn. He also gave land for the building of Aberconwy abbey. He died at Aberconwy abbey on 11 April 1240, and was buried there. There is a statue of Llywelyn the Great on the square at Conwy, and Joan's stone tomb is in Beaumaris church.

Cricieth castle

Statue of Llywelyn the Great, Conwy

Castell y Bere

Dolbadarn castle

Joan's coffin in Beaumaris church

Why was Llywelyn the Great important?

- ♛ Llywelyn the Great was one of the most powerful princes of Wales.
- ♛ He wanted to have one single Welsh principality.
- ♛ He built more stone castles than any other prince before him.
- ♛ He gave generously to the church.
- ♛ He was an inspiration to his grandson, Llywelyn ap Gruffudd (p. 51).

Some of the Main Welsh Castles

Deganwy

Denbigh

Ewloe

Dolbadarn

Dolwyddelan

Rhodwydd-yn-Iâl

Cricieth

Deudraeth

Dinas Brân

Madrun

Prysor

Carndochan

Mathrafal

Y Bere

Dolforwyn

Aberystwyth

Ystradmeurig

Llanrhystud

Castell Hywel

Cardigan

Nevern

Dinefwr

Dryslwyn

Carreg Cennen

Dolwyddelan castle

Gruffudd ap Llywelyn

Prisoner in the Tower of London, 1244

It was St David's Day 1244, and Gruffudd ap Llywelyn had been a prisoner in the Tower of London for three long years.

Things could be worse, he thought for the hundredth time. At least Henry III had arranged for him to stay in a room, instead of in a cold damp cell. His eldest son Owain was a prisoner too, but they were allowed to see each other every now and then. His wife Senena and his other sons were allowed to visit them both. It was such a pleasure to speak Welsh to them and to forget his miserable circumstances, if only for a while.

It was all the fault of Dafydd, his half-brother. Dafydd had stolen the lands that Llywelyn the Great, Gruffudd's father, had given him in Gwynedd. Even worse, he had captured Gruffudd and handed him over as hostage to Henry III.

Henry had come to speak to him once or twice. He had come in his royal robes, as if to rub salt into the wound and break Gruffudd's heart. 'I'll help you return to Wales,' was his promise. 'And I'll help you regain your lands.' But Gruffudd doubted it. After all, he and Owain were a great threat to the king. Dafydd had no sons, so after his death, Gruffudd or Owain would be prince of Wales. No, Henry was in no hurry to free them.

Gruffudd had reached the end of his tether. He couldn't stay in the Tower for the rest of his life. He had to escape, return to Gwynedd and challenge Dafydd. He had already thought up a plan, and now was the time to put it into action.

He tore the sheets from the bed and the curtains from the window. He knotted them together to make a long rope, tied one end to the leg of the bed, and dropped the other end out of the window.

Gruffudd waited a moment, in case a guard had spotted the rope. But there was no sound from outside. He leaned out of the window. There was no one in sight. So he turned, caught hold of the rope and climbed out backwards. Slowly he slid down, hand over hand. Then he paused.

He had heard a noise that sent a chill down his spine. The sound of tearing cloth. The rope wasn't strong enough!

It was all over in an instant: Gruffudd fell from the Tower and died as he hit the ground below.

Why was Gruffudd ap Llywelyn important?

- ♛ Gruffudd ap Llywelyn was the father of Llywelyn ap Gruffudd, or Llywelyn II (known as 'Our Last Leader') (p. 51).
- ♛ His story shows how the sons of Welsh princes fought each other for their father's lands.

Gruffudd ap Llywelyn was the son of Llywelyn the Great and Tangwystl. After Llywelyn the Great married Joan (p. 46), Dafydd, Joan's son, became the official heir.

Gruffudd was handed over to King John in 1211, and was kept hostage till 1215. Llywelyn the Great gave Gruffudd a lot of land, but in 1228 he took back the land and imprisoned him for six years. In 1238 his brother Dafydd captured him and handed him over as hostage to Henry III. He was imprisoned in the Tower of London, and while trying to escape in 1244, he fell to his death. He had many sons, Owain, Llywelyn, Dafydd and Rhodri. The two most famous are Llywelyn ap Gruffudd and Dafydd ap Gruffudd (p. 51).

Llywelyn ap Gruffudd (Llywelyn II)
Treachery in the Bell Tower, 1282

A gang of men had gathered in the bell tower of Bangor Cathedral. But they weren't there to ring the bells. It was nearly midnight on a frosty night at the beginning of December 1282. Anyone with any sense was in bed keeping warm. The only sound was the hooting of owls – or the whispers of the men. Even if you'd listened hard, you'd have heard very little of that secret conversation. Maybe a word or two would have reached your ears: "Lure Llywelyn somewhere far from Snowdonia", "Get rid of him", "Let his brother Dafydd take over". Yes, something strange was afoot in the bell tower of Bangor Cathedral. The followers of Llywelyn ap Gruffudd, prince of Wales, were planning to betray him.

Bangor cathedral

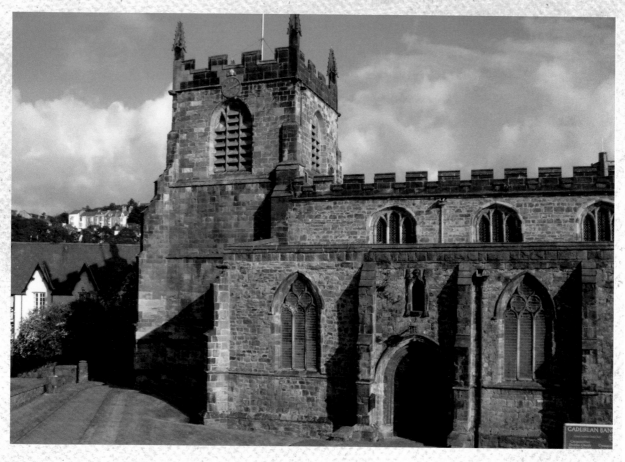

Llywelyn ap Gruffudd
The killing of Llywelyn, 'the Last Leader'

A few weeks later, on the 11th of December, 1282, Llywelyn ap Gruffudd was riding through a forest at Cilmeri, near Builth. He and his soldiers were going to the aid of his brother, Dafydd, who was resisting the forces of Edward I, king of England.

The ground was steep, and a coating of snow made it very slippery. Llywelyn dismounted and carefully led his horse along a path that followed the river Irfon.

It was the end of the year, and Llywelyn was casting his mind back over the past twelve months. 1282 had not been a happy year for him. In June his wife Eleanor had died in childbirth. Llywelyn thought the world of their baby daughter Gwenllïan, but he still missed his wife.

He felt rather weary. Llywelyn was now 57 years old, and for the past 30 years he'd been fighting against the English: the Marcher Lords and Edward I, and also against the Welsh: Gruffudd ap Gwenwynwyn from Powys and

his own brothers Owain, Dafydd and Rhodri. If Llywelyn and his three brothers had only joined forces, they would have defeated Edward long ago. But his brothers didn't want Llywelyn to be prince. Rhodri and Dafydd had supported Edward I, and as a reward the king had given Rhodri lands in England. But Dafydd was the dangerous one. Llywelyn knew that Dafydd had plotted to murder him back in 1274, and he was still wary of him.

The woods were quiet and Llywelyn noticed that he had only a small band of soldiers around him. Where had the others gone? He gripped his sword hilt as he led his horse. He felt in his bones that something was wrong.

Suddenly a large body of English troops appeared and charged at the Welsh. As they clashed, shouts rang out. One soldier ran towards Llywelyn with his spear at the ready. Llywelyn let go of his horse,

unsheathed his sword and faced up to him. Sword rang against spear as Llywelyn fought for his life. But the soldier was too strong and too fast; he ran his spear through Llywelyn and killed him.

The soldier who killed Llywelyn was a Shropshire man. His name was Stephen de Frankton. He was very pleased to have killed a Welshman, because there was a reward of one shilling (5p) for a Welshman's head, and a shilling was lot of money to a poor soldier. So he hacked off the head and showed it to the soldiers who were coming up behind him. Drops of bright red blood fell on the white snow. As yet, Stephen de Frankton did not realise that he had killed the last Prince of Wales at Cilmeri.

* * *

News of the death of Llywelyn spread throughout Wales. The monks of Cwm-hir abbey collected Llywelyn's body and buried it in their grounds. But the English, once they'd realised that the dead man was Llywelyn, kept his head and sent it to Edward I in London. Edward ordered that the head be put on a pole and paraded around the city. Then, Llywelyn's head was placed on the Tower of London, where, in his youth, his own father had fallen to his death.

No-one in Wales could believe it. Llywelyn ap Gruffudd dead? The Prince of Wales slaughtered? Shortly after Llywelyn's death, there was a violent storm, and the people of Wales thought the world was coming to an end. It was as if the whole country had been crushed.

Llywelyn ap Gruffudd
(Llywelyn, 'Our Last Leader') (1225–82)

Llywelyn ap Gruffudd had many titles: Prince of Aberffraw, Lord of Eryri and Prince of Wales. He was the son of Gruffudd ap Llywelyn (p. 50) and Senena. Llywelyn had to fight his brothers Owain, Rhodri and Dafydd, for their lands in Gwynedd.

1255: He defeated Owain and Dafydd, and kept Owain prisoner in Dolbadarn Castle for twenty years.

1256–8: Llywelyn was sole ruler of Gwynedd Uwch Conwy. He captured the lands of Perfeddwlad (a large part of the present-day counties of Denbigh and Flint) and most of the lands of the Welsh princes.

1258: Llywelyn called himself prince of Wales for the first time.

Early 1260s: He captured a lot of territory in the March.

1267: He made a treaty with King Henry III in Montgomery (p. 54). He was recognised as prince of Wales and promised to pay 25,000 marks (over £16,000) to the king for ten years.

1272: After the death of Henry III, Llywelyn refused to recognise the new king, Edward I. He also refused to pay the money that had been promised. Dafydd and Rhodri supported King Edward, and Rhodri (the grandfather of Owain Lawgoch, p. 64) was rewarded with lands in England.

1274: His brother Dafydd and Gruffudd ap Gwenwynwyn of Powys plotted to kill him. The plot failed and both plotters fled to England to King Edward I.

1276: Edward I waged war against Llywelyn. He managed to capture Anglesey, which produced a lot of wheat for the prince of Wales.

1277: Llywelyn made a treaty with Edward I at Aberconwy (p. 55). He lost a lot of his land but kept the title Prince of Wales.

1278: Llywelyn married Eleanor de Montfort in Worcester Cathedral. Edward I paid for the wedding feast and gave the bride away.

1282: Dafydd started the final war against Edward I. Llywelyn did not join in immediately, but did so after the death of his wife Eleanor on June 19, as she gave birth to their daughter, Gwenllïan. On 11 December 1282, Llywelyn was killed at Cilmeri near Builth Wells. His head was cut off and sent to Edward I in London. Llywelyn's body was buried in the abbey of Cwm-hir (see map on p. 42).

Why was Llywelyn ap Gruffudd important?

- ♛ Llywelyn ap Gruffudd was the last prince of Wales – known as 'our Last Leader' (*'ein Llyw Olaf'*).
- ♛ He was the first and last prince to be recognised as Prince of Wales by England.
- ♛ For a while he managed to unite the Welsh under one prince, and Welsh people became more aware of being one nation.

Llywelyn's memorial, Cilmeri

GER Y FAN HON
Y LLADDWYD
LLYWELYN
EIN LLYW OLAF
1282

The tablet on Llywelyn's memorial, Cilmeri
['Llywelyn, Our Last Leader, was killed nearby in 1282']

The Treaty of Montgomery 1267

Chest

Hawarden

**GWYNEDD
Uwch Conwy**

Is Conwy

**Powys
Fadog** ③

**Powys
Wenwynwyn** ④

Cedewain
⑤

Montgomery

Ceri

Llywelyn's Castles
1. Aberffraw
2. Aber
3. Dinas Brân
4. Mathrafal
5. Dolforwyn
6. Dinefwr
7. Caerphilly

Ceredigion

Gwrtheyrnion

Maelienydd

Builth

Elfael

Cardigan

Emlyn

Cantref Mawr

Cantref Bychan

Carmarthen
⑥

Brecon

Afan

Glynrhondda

Meisgyn

Senghennydd

Gwynllwg

Caerleon

⑦

	Territories ruled by Llywelyn ap Gruffudd
	Territories of the English King
	Territories of the Marcher Lords

The Treaty of Aberconwy 1277

ABERCONWY

GWYNEDD Uwch Conwy

Y Berfeddwlad

● **Cheste**

Montgomery

Penweddig

Builth

Cardigan

Carmarthen

These two maps show just how much land Llywelyn – and the princes whom he ruled – lost to Henry III, Edward I and the lords of the Marches. By the Treaty of Rhuddlan in 1284 (after Llywelyn's death) more of the Welsh peoples land came under the control of the English.

'Excellent news, your Highness! Dafydd ap Gruffudd, brother of Llywelyn, has been captured at Castell y Bere and executed in Shrewsbury.'

Edward I thanked his servant for the news, and gave a gloating smile. That treacherous rogue Dafydd deserved his fate: to be hung, drawn and quartered. After the death of his brother, Llywelyn, Dafydd had only lasted as prince for six months!

Things were going very well for Edward. He'd managed to conquer Wales at last. He drew out a map of the new counties and set it on the table before him. What a pleasure it had been to divide Gwynedd into three counties and Deheubarth into two counties. The Welsh would soon forget their old kingdoms.

He had great plans for the country. The plans would cost a fortune, but would be worth every penny. He was determined to keep the Welsh under control, and castles were the answer. He had already built and strengthened many castles – at Aberystwyth, Flint, Rhuddlan and Builth – but more were needed, especially in Gwynedd. Edward ran his finger along the coastline from Conwy to Beaumaris, from Caernarfon across to Harlech. Yes, he would put his plan in motion, as soon as possible.

Edward reached for a piece of bread from his silver plate. He took great delight in eating from this plate every day, because it was made of Llywelyn's silver. Edward smiled at the thought of all the treasure he'd captured in Gwynedd, Llywelyn's crown, of course, and Y Groes Naid, the sacred jewelled cross of the princes of Gwynedd, which contained a piece of the cross on which Jesus had died.

But he still had one problem the fate of Wales' greatest treasure, Gwenllïan, daughter of Llywelyn ap Gruffudd. Edward had snatched her after the death of Llywelyn. She was now a year old and still at the court. Edward could not murder a baby, but he had to make sure that she would never marry and give birth to sons. He didn't want to have to fight another prince of Wales.

He called one of his advisers and asked his opinion.

'That's no problem, your Highness,' said the adviser. 'Send her to the nunnery in Sempringham in Lincolnshire. No one will ever find her there. She'll be far enough from Wales and surrounded by high stone walls.'

'An excellent idea,' said Edward. 'We'll do it this week. Of course she won't be taught a word of Welsh, only English and Latin. Her father, Llywelyn, would turn in his grave if he knew!' And Edward laughed heartily.

Gwenllïan was born in June, 1282. Her mother, Eleanor, died while giving birth to her. The child was six months old when her father, Llywelyn ap Gruffudd was killed. She was captured by Edward I, king of England. Edward did not want any sons to be born to Llywelyn's line, so he sent Gwenllïan to Sempringham Priory in Lincolnshire to be a nun.

Gwenllïan was one of 200 nuns who lived there. No one was allowed to visit the nuns, and the priory was encircled by a stone wall. Gwenllïan died at the age of 54.

Since 1993 there has been a memorial to Gwenllïan at Sempringham. The first memorial was vandalised. The present memorial is a boulder from Penmaenmawr quarry. The boulder happens to be in the shape of a nun.

In 1996 the Princess Gwenllïan Society was formed. A plaque in her memory has been placed on the summit of Snowdon, and a nearby mountain named after her.

Gwenllïan's memorial in Sempringham

Caernarfon castle

Harlech castle

The Statute of Rhuddlan 1284

The Principality
Other Crown Lands
Lands of the Marcher Lords
Government Headquarters
Castle

ANGLESEY
Beaumaris
Conwy
Bangor
Caernarfon
Rhuddlan
Flint
Denbigh
Chester
Rhuthun
Bromfield and Yale
Chirk
Shrewsbury
COUNTY OF CAERNARFON
Cricieth
Harlech
COUNTY OF MEIRIONNYDD
POWYS
MONTGOMERY
Ludlow
Aberystwyth
COUNTY OF CARDIGAN
Cardigan
Newcastle Emlyn
PEMBROKE
St Davids
COUNTY OF CARMARTHEN
Builth (Llanfair-ym-Muallt)
Hereford
Haverfordwest
St Clears
Carmarthen
BRECON
Abergavenny
Pembroke
Cydweli
Swansea
GOWER
GLAMORGAN
Cardiff

Moving from Llan-faes

Anglesey, 1301

The worst day of my life so far. And I'm only twelve years old!

Knock! Knock! Knock! That's how we were woken up this morning. Not just us, but the whole village. A soldier from the town of Beaumaris was on the doorstep, ordering us to move house.

"What? Move house? When do you want us to move?" asked my father sleepily.

"Saturday!" shouted the soldier. "And if you haven't moved by midday Saturday, we'll force you out."

"But where to? And why?" My father was awake at last.

"Not far – only twelve miles away to Newborough, or Rhosyr, as you Welsh call it," snapped the soldier.

"What? Move twelve miles away? It'll take us a week and more to move everything. And why should we go? There's good farming land here." Father was shouting by now.

"The king has plans. You'll hear about them in due course. Anyway, you've no choice. You've got to go." The soldier reached for his sword threateningly.

It took us a while to realise what was happening. My mother started to cry, as did all of us children. We were all so happy in Llan-faes. It was a prosperous town and my father used to fish from the busy harbour. What right did they have to move us?

"I was afraid this would happen," said my father sadly. "I'd heard that Edward I wanted to move the market and the fairs from here to Beaumaris. Now I suppose the Englishmen from the town will take our land and use it for their crops and their livestock. The Welsh have been too rebellious – in Caernarfon and Conwy – so they're making us move as far away as possible."

Over the past few years we children had watched the building of Beaumaris Castle and the town around. We'd seen one thousand five hundred men dig a deep moat, bring rocks from Penmon quarry and put them in place. They were all Englishmen, and came from every county in England, so they said. We'd watched the king's boats bring in wood, lead and other materials from Chester. And we'd watched the castle take shape – the four big towers at each corner, joined by a thick wall. I remember the big strong door, with the iron bars, being put in place. Then came the portcullis with the spikes hanging down, the drawbridge across the moat, and the high wall around the whole town. The castle and town walls were whitewashed to make them sparkle in the sunlight.

It wasn't long before all the English came and settled in the town. Then every Welsh family was ordered to send one member to town each week to buy and sell goods. The English fixed the prices, and made us pay a tax on everything. It was a pain having to carry all the goods to town: the milk, cheese, butter, honey, wheat, wool and skins, and to drive all the animals there as well. Before, we used to buy and sell amongst ourselves, but we weren't allowed to do that any more.

And now, on top of everything, we had to move – in a few days! Luckily we had few belongings, but even so we had to go back and forth many times to collect our furniture, and our few animals. My mother broke her heart when she saw the soldiers setting fire to all the houses just as we were leaving for the last time.

My father grumbled loudly as we turned towards Newborough, with the smoke from our old house in our nostrils:

"Things are going from bad to worse for us. The English are the only ones who are allowed to work or own land in town. We're not allowed to speak Welsh, nor carry arms. They steal our land, and walk the boundary each year, to make sure we can't get it back. They're trying to push us out of our own country, that's what they're doing."

My poor father! And poor old us. King Edward I has just given the title of Prince of Wales to his son Edward, who's in Lincoln in England. Will we ever have a Welsh prince of Wales again? Since the death of Llywelyn, our Last Leader, life has been so unkind to us.

Beaumaris castle

Laugharne – Beating the Bounds

The people of Laugharne walk along the boundary – or beat the bounds - of their town every three years, usually at the end of May. They have been doing so for centuries.

The walk is mentioned in the town's records that go back to 1711. But the custom is much older than that. The town was granted an official charter in 1290, and the townspeople believe that the custom of beating the bounds dates at least from that time.

In the old days there were no maps to show who owned land, so people would walk along the boundary to prove ownership. Laugharne was a Norman town, with an impressive castle, and this was how its inhabitants showed the Welsh that they were the owners.

The boundary of Laugharne is quite long, 22 to 24 miles, and the walk starts early in the morning, at 6.30. The entire walk takes about 9 hours, so some people, including children, only walk part of the way.

Landowners and residents of Laugharne beating the bounds in 1948

Llywelyn Bren

Rebellion, 1316

"Llywelyn, why are you looking so miserable?" asked his wife one morning in the autumn of 1315. "You haven't been happy since the king sent Lord de Turberville to Glamorgan."

"You're quite right. I haven't," replied Llywelyn, Lord of Senghennydd. "Turberville is a cruel, cunning man. He's been stealing my land. I try to remind myself how lucky I am. I still have some land left, and plenty of animals, books and gold jewellery. But things aren't looking good for

us Welsh. Turberville has removed Welshmen from important posts and replaced them with his own men. They haven't shown any sympathy towards us Welsh." Llywelyn suddenly fell silent and rested his head on his hands.

"What's wrong?" said his wife worriedly. "What is it?"

"I've decided that something's got to be done. Something decisive. We've got to hit back, fight, rebel." Llywelyn raised his head. He looked anxious but determined.

"Oh Llywelyn," said his wife. "Rebellion? That's a very big step to take. But I agree, we can't go on living under the Englishman's thumb. Someone must do something about it, and you are the most powerful lord in this area."

* * *

During the winter of 1315, Llywelyn began plotting in earnest. He contacted men who were willing to fight, laid up a store of arms – and prepared for war!

On 28 January 1316, Llywelyn, with a huge army of 10,000 men, attacked Caerphilly Castle. This was a strong well-built fortress, with a rampart and a huge moat, but Llywelyn and his men captured it and burnt the town to the ground. On they went to the Vale of Glamorgan and to Cardiff – the rebellion was a great success.

But then, bad news reached Llywelyn and his army. The Earl of Hereford was marching towards them with a large force of Englishmen. Llywelyn ordered everyone to flee to the hills and caves of Glamorgan. There they avoided the English for several weeks. But in the end, with the enemy closing in on them near Ystradfellte, Llywelyn decided it was time to surrender. He himself took the message to the English soldiers. He didn't want his men to suffer, but preferred to die in their stead.

Llywelyn was imprisoned in the Tower of London for a while, and his lands and his property were given to the English crown. His property included a suit of armour, a pair of metal gauntlets, a golden ornament, ten gold rings, Welsh manuscripts and one French manuscript.

In 1318, he was moved to Cardiff Castle. King Edward II was determined to punish him cruelly, as a warning to the Welsh not to rebel. Llywelyn was dragged through the streets of Cardiff, and then hung, drawn and quartered.

But Llywelyn Bren had had his wish. His fellow-Welshmen went unpunished. In his own words:

"It is better for one man to die, than for a whole nation to perish by the sword."

Caerphilly castle

Llywelyn Bren may have been the great-grandson of Ifor Bach (p. 30). He was Lord of Senghennydd and owned a lot of land and property in the uplands of Glamorgan – around 600 sheep and 1,000 cattle. He led a rebellion in Glamorgan against the officers of King Edward II who were stealing land and jobs from the Welsh. The story tells of the last years of his life, from 1315 to his death in 1318.

Why was Llywelyn Bren important?

♛ Llywelyn led an important rebellion against the king's officers, who were trying to steal land from the Welsh at that time.

Life wasn't easy for the Welsh in the fourteenth century. Had there been a newspaper at the time, these would have been the headlines:

1317: Cold wet weather. The harvest has failed again! For three years we've had dreadful weather. It's been so cold and so wet. To make matters worse, the harvest has failed three times in a row: in 1315, last year, and again this year! The price of wheat is rising and all foodstuffs are expensive.

1349: The Black Plague is still with us – more and more people are dying!

One third – yes, one third – of all the inhabitants of Wales have died since 1847, the year when the plague first struck. You know the symptoms: sneezing, followed by ugly blisters and black swellings all over the body. Within three or four days two things can happen – either you get better, or your whole body turns black and you die.

No one wants to care for the sick, so they're left on their own to die. The bodies are buried together in huge pits.

The situation is dire – there aren't enough people left to work in the fields or care for the livestock. No one goes to the fairs or the markets in case they catch the plague. Some think that the plague is God's punishment. What will become of us?

The poets of the time spread the news, just as journalists do today. Here is part of the sad lament of Llywelyn Fychan on the death of some of his children from the plague:

Y nod a ddug eneidiau . . . dwyn Iwan wiwlan ei wedd ymlaen y lleill naw mlynedd: . . . dwyn Morfudd, dwyn Dafydd deg, dwyn Ieuan, llon degan llu, dwyn â didawddgwyn Dyddgu, a'm gadaw, frad oerfraw fryd, yn freiddfyw, mewn afrwyddfyd.	[The mark of the plague took lives . . . took Iwan, fair of face, who was nine years older than the rest: . . . took Morfudd, took sweet Dafydd, took Ieuan, who loved to play, took the carefree Dyddgu, and left me, how cruel that is, half alive in a harsh world.]

Poetry to Remember

The poets of the Age of Princes used to write verses to commemorate important events. A poem can bring to life the feelings of people at the time. The pupils at Ysgol Felinheli have written a poem about an important battle that took place in their area. Why not write a poem about an important event in your life or in the life of your family?

Moel y Don

The winter snow is cold in Moel y Don
But there's comfort in the hills, though
summer's gone,
We've gathered in the corn,
The mill awaits the dawn
And a little peace reigns over Moel y Don.

The smoke is dead black over Moel y Don,
Each cottage, barn and haystack one by one
Is being set alight;
Our people live in fright
Of grim starvation here in Moel y Don.

They've built a makeshift bridge at Moel y Don,
By lashing boats together one by one.
And down there by the Straits
A mighty army waits;
The coast is trembling down at Moel y Don.

Resistance is the word at Moel y Don,
The longbows and the spears are poised as one,
And with the rising tide
From woods on either side
Fly Welshmen's flaming arrows at Moel y Don.

Blood turned the Menai red at Moel y Don,
And soon the Normans fled from Moel y Don;
Old Arfon's rocky shield
Was never going to yield,
And victory was ours at Moel y Don.

Poem by pupils of year 6, Ysgol Felinheli, with Myrddin ap Dafydd (trans. Geraint Løvgreen)

Moel y Don is on the banks of the Menai Straits, a narrow stretch of sea that separates Anglesey from Arfon. In the days of Llywelyn II, a large English army attacked Anglesey and stole the wheat harvest. At that time the whole of Gwynedd depended on Anglesey wheat. That's why Anglesey was known as the 'Mother of Wales' (Môn Mam Cymru). The English set about building a bridge of boats, so that their best horsemen and their powerful horses could cross to attack Arfon. But the Welsh hiding in the woods at Port Dinorwic (Y Felinheli) saw what was happening. Their arrows rained down on the English troops and killed many of them. As the men panicked and tried to escape, half the army and their valuable horses were drowned in the strong tide. And Gwynedd was safe once again.

Owain Lawgoch (Redhand)

A Prince in France, 1378

It was almost daybreak on a summer's morning in the town of Mortagne-sur-Gironde in the South of France. Owain Lawgoch hadn't slept very well, because the night was so hot. He was one of a band of mercenary soldiers who were fighting for Charles, King of France. The soldiers were laying siege to the town, so that no-one could go in or out.

Owain had got up early, put on a thin shirt and a light cloak, and had gone to look across at the town's castle in case there was trouble afoot. With luck, the people under siege would soon be starving and ready to surrender to the king.

Owain was accompanied by one man. He was called John Lamb and was either Scottish or English. John Lamb had only recently joined the company and Owain had taken to him at once, because he had brought a message from Wales. He liked to hear about Wales, because he was a Welshman and an important one at that. His grandfather, Rhodri, was the brother of Llywelyn II. And John Lamb's message was important – the whole of Wales wanted Owain to return home. They wanted to make him prince, and John Lamb said he would be prepared to help him.

Since then John had been a good friend to Owain. Owain had often told him of his two attempts to return to Wales. The first attempt had been in 1369, when the weather was too stormy. On the second occasion, in 1372, the king of France had recalled him from Guernsey, because he had work for him to do. For his part, John would describe the situation in Wales. He would tell of the Second Plague that had killed so many, of the heavy taxes that the Welsh had to pay to the English, and of the poets who still sang of Owain returning to Wales to lead a rebellion.

All was quiet at Mortagne castle that morning in July. Owain suddenly remembered that he had not combed his hair, so he turned to John and asked him to fetch him his comb. While he waited, the tall, handome Owain watched the sun rise slowly over the castle tower. It would be another fine day.

Owain heard John's footsteps approach. He's back already with my comb, he thought. But as well as a comb, John had a small spear in his hand. John Lamb was not a friend, but an assassin hired by the English to kill Owain, so that there would be no-one left to lead the Welsh. He stabbed Owain several times, till he was certain he was dead. For that he could claim a twenty pound reward, a fortune at the time. Then John Lamb sneaked away, leaving Owain Lawgoch, the last heir of Gwynedd, lying dead in a French town.

Owain Lawgoch's seal

Owain Lawgoch
(died 1378)

Owain's grandfather, Rhodri, was the brother of Llywelyn II. Owain Lawgoch (Owain ap Tomos ap Rhodri) was the last of the line of the princes of Gwynedd. He was born around 1340, but went to France when he was quite young. When his father died in 1363, he returned to Britain only to find that the King had taken his lands in England, Llŷn and Mechain. He went back to France and led a band of mercenary soldiers who fought for the French king. The French called him Yvain de Galles. He tried to return to Wales in 1369 to claim his lands, but was driven back by a storm. He tried again in 1372, and was lent ships and money by the king of France. He got as far as the island of Guernsey, before being summoned by the king to do other work for him.

He fought in many places before arriving at Mortagne-sur-Gironde in 1378. A Scotsman caled John Lamb joined the band of soldiers. He had been hired by the English to kill Owain Lawgoch, and prevent his ever leading a Welsh rebellion. Owain Lawgoch was killed by John Lamb on 22 July 1378. He was buried at Saint Léger on the banks of the river Garonne. But the Welsh kept hoping that he was still alive. According to the legend that grew up around him, he was asleep in a cave, waiting for the call to lead his people.

In 2003 there was a ceremony to remember Owain Lawgoch at Mortagne-sur-Gironde. 2,000 people, both Welsh and French, witnessed the unveiling of a special memorial. Welsh soil was scattered around the memorial, and daffodils from St David's were planted at the spot.

Owain Lawgoch's memorial, Mortagne-sur-Gironde

The ceremony to unveil Owain Lawgoch's memorial in 2003

Let's Make a Catapult

In the Age of the Princes, a catapult was used to throw fireballs and rocks at people and property. Here is a simple catapult. You could use it to throw **marshmallows** or **table tennis balls**. But **never** aim a catapult at anyone else.

Look at the picture and follow the instructions. Allow time for the glue to dry between each step.

Place a length of wood about **15cm x 7cm** on a table. Use wood glue (PVA) to stick a wooden clothes peg along its length. Wait for the glue to dry, then glue a cube of wood **3cm x 3cm** onto the open end of the clothes peg. When that has dried, stick another piece of wood about **2cm x 19cm** onto the cube. Then glue a plastic bottle top (e.g. a milk bottle top) to the strip of wood, allowing enough room at the very end for you to press down with your fingers and fire the catapult.

CONQUER THE CASTLE – a catapult game

How about building a motte and bailey castle on the beach and bombarding it with your catapult?

1. Build a motte and bailey castle – Dig a round ditch, and pile up the sand from the ditch to form a mound (bailey) in the middle. On the mound, build a castle using a castle-shaped bucket, or an ordinary bucket.

2. Attack the castle with the catapult – Place a piece of seaweed or a ball of wet sand on the catapult and 'fire'. If the seaweed or ball of sand lands on the castle, that's counted as a 'hit'. Once you've made 10 hits, you have conquered the castle.

Let's Design Costumes

Let's design costumes – for men and women - from the Age of the Princes. You could do this on paper or on the computer. There are plenty of ideas in this book, or you could look for pictures on the web.

Look closely at the colours of the costumes, and also the combination of colours.

Or how about designing a modern costume, using elements of the costumes of the Age of the Princes? Decide on the style features that are typical of the period – e.g. wide sleeves for women.

Owain Glyndŵr

Owain's Court in Sycharth, 1390

Two poets, called Iolo Goch and Gruffudd Llwyd, were walking through the village of Llansilin in Powys. It was late afternoon on a fine day in early spring. The trees were almost in leaf and the birds were chirping and singing sweetly. The two men were on their way to Owain Glyndŵr's court in Sycharth. They were going to perform their verses at a special banquet that very evening.

"I do enjoy going to Sycharth," said Iolo Goch. "It's such a beautiful place, set on a hill with a moat around it. The building is in the form of a cross, like a church, and even has a bell tower. The roof is covered in brightly coloured tiles instead of thatch – can you believe that? – and there's coloured glass in the windows."

"That's amazing!" said Gruffudd Llwyd. "This will be my first visit. It sounds a very modern place, but then Owain Glyndŵr and his wife Marged are rich, aren't they? So they can afford far more than the common people."

"Of course they can," said Iolo Goch. "They don't have to live under the same roof as their animals, as the rest of us do! In fact there are loads of rooms in the court: a great hall, bedrooms, a kitchen, a chapel, and even a lavatory. And there are plenty of oak cupboards to hold clothes, food, dishes and kitchen equipment."

"I've heard that Owain brews his own beer," said Gruffudd Llwyd.

"He does indeed, and a fine beer it is too. No-one is ever thirsty in Sycharth," said Iolo Goch with a chuckle. "The bread is delicious – the grain from the wheat fields is milled in Sycharth mill. There's a vineyard and an orchard in the grounds too, as well as a fishpond and a dovecote. So there's never any shortage of food and drink. Look!" He pointed. "There it is, Gruffudd. We're almost there. Can you see the deer in the parkland?"

"Yes, I can," replied Gruffudd. "And some other small animals. Rabbits!"

"I can see them too!" said Iolo Goch, who was getting more and more excited. "D'you know, I've written a special poem – a cywydd – in praise of Sycharth, and I'm going to perform it for the first time tonight."

"Does Owain know?" asked Gruffudd.

"No, I hope it'll be a big surprise," said Iolo. "The name of the poem is 'Owain Glyndŵr's Court in Sycharth'."

"I've got a new poem for Owain too," said Gruffudd Llwyd. "In the poem I call him the Son of Prophecy, the one who will come and lead our nation against the English. I want to remind him how important he is to Wales. After all, he comes from the line of the princes of Powys and Deheubarth. Since Owain Lawgoch was murdered, Owain Glyndŵr is the best hope of the Welsh."

"That's right," agreed Iolo Goch. "Owain must realise that we are relying on him in these dark days. That's why I feel it's important to praise Sycharth and describe it in detail – to tell everyone how the door is always open and every visitor is given a gift."

"Perhaps we'll have gifts in exchange for our verses," said Gruffudd.

"We probably will. But look, the sun is beginning to set. Hurry up or the banquet will have started without us," said Iolo, and they both laughed merrily.

Sycharth today

Main hall

Deer park

Gatehouse

Drawbridge

Motte

Watermill

Vegetable garden

Barracks and stables

Brewery

Hen-house

Crop fields

Moat

Dovecot

Vineyard

Orchard

Castles in the Age of Owain Glyndŵr
(around 1359–1416)

Owain Glyndŵr was Lord of the estates of Glyndyfrdwy (Corwen) and Cynllaith (Powys). He had land in Ceredigion too. He was related to the princes of Powys Fadog on his father's side, and to the princes of Deheubarth on his mother's side. His wife, Marged, came from the line of the princes of Gwynedd, and was the daughter of Sir David Hanmer, a famous judge.

Owain is said to have studied law in London, and fought for the English against the French. He was quite rich, as proven by Iolo Goch's description of his court in Sycharth.

Although Owain Glyndŵr was a nobleman who seemed happy enough to live in Wales under English rule, we shall see in the following pages that he was in fact dissatisfied with the situation in his home country.

Key:

- **Castles captured by Owain**
- **Some other Welsh castles** (Owain laid siege to many of them)
- **The main battles of the war**

Beaumaris
Conwy
Rhuddlan
Flint
Denbigh
Caernarfon
Rhuthun
Dolwyddelan
Glyndyfrdwy
Cricieth
Chirk
Harlech
Sycharth
Welshpool
Hyddgen (1401)
Montgomery
Aberystwyth
Brynglas (1402)
Painscastle
Cardigan
Newcastle Emlyn
Hay
Cilgerran
Grosmont (1405)
Dryslwyn
Aberhonddu
Haverfordwest
Dinefwr
Carmarthen
Carreg Cennen
Abergavenny
Laugharne
Cydweli
Pwllmelyn (1405)
Tenby
Pembroke
Swansea
Coety
Cardiff

the BUGLE

16 September 1400

THE PROCLAMATION OF A PRINCE AT GLYNDYFRDWY

Today three hundred Welshmen came to Glyndyfrdwy, between Corwen and Llangollen, to proclaim Lord Glyndyfrdwy, or Owain Glynd?r, prince of Wales. Owain Glynd?r is descended from the royal families of Powys and Deheubarth, and his wife belongs to the royal family of Gwynedd. The poets say that the Church. Welsh students at Oxford are supporting Owain. Just recently the English rose against them, shouting, 'Kill them! Kill the Welsh dogs!' We've all had quite enough of the present situation. We are on the march. Watch out, Henry IV!'

We think that Crach Ffinnant 'prophet'. He has prophesied that Owain Glynd?r will lead the Welsh to a great victory against the English, and Owain believes him.

No one from King Henry IV's camp would comment when The Bugle contacted the court yesterday.

Owain Glyndŵr at Dolwyddelan Castle

Glyndŵr's Rebellion
The rebellion begins! Rhuthun, 18 September 1400

"Why have I got to have Reginald Grey as a neighbour?" complained Owain Glyndŵr to his men, one night at his court in Glyndyfrdwy. "He's the neighbour from hell."

Reginald Grey, Lord of the Vale of Clwyd, had been a thorn in Owain's side for some time. The two were neighbours, but there were always disputes between them, usually involving land.

"He's been stealing my land again!" said Owain angrily. "This time it's land near Bryneglwys. The king knows that I own the land, but he won't support me against that damned Englishman!"

Owain jumped to his feet in a fury. He was a tall, powerful man, and his blue eyes were flashing. He tugged at his beard, and turned to his men.

"It's time to take action, men. We'll start the rebellion, and at the same time teach a lesson to that Reginald Grey in his castle in Rhuthun. It's market day in Rhuthun tomorrow. We'll gather just outside the town before dawn. Let our supporters know."

Early next morning, Owain Glyndŵr and three hundred of his men gathered outside the town of Rhuthun. As soon as the gate was open, they attacked. The Welsh burst in carrying flaming torches. Rhuthun was burnt to the ground in no time, and the townspeople ran for their lives. Apparently only one building – 2 Well Street – was still left standing.

There were only a few soldiers guarding the town, but there were more at the castle, and the Welsh failed to gain access. But it didn't matter. The army went on to burn more English towns that week: Denbigh, Rhuddlan, Flint, Hawarden, Holt, Oswestry and Welshpool.

Henry IV was alarmed. The Welsh had been fairly quiet after the murder of Owain Lawgoch. He hoped they'd decided to keep the peace and accept English rule. Now he had no choice but to take his troops to north Wales to impose order. Eight Welshmen were caught and hanged. The body of one of them – Gronw ap Tudur – was quartered, and a piece sent to each of four boroughs in Wales. Henry IV wanted to show that the English were still in control of Wales.

But the rest of Owain Glyndŵr's army disappeared over the winter months. They had taken to the hills, where they would wait for the next chance to attack. Glyndŵr's rebellion had begun.

Glyndŵr's Rebellion

The Capture of Conwy Castle – Good Friday, 1 April 1401

It was early Good Friday morning, and the bell of Conwy church was ringing out. In the castle the soldiers of the garrison prepared to march out to the church for the Easter service. Soon the castle gate opened, and out they came – 50 armed men and 60 archers. As soon as they'd gone, the two guards, who were left behind, set about closing the gate carefully.

A short distance from Conwy castle 40 armed men were hiding. Their leaders were two brothers from Anglesey – Rhys and Gwilym ap Tudur. They saw the gate open … and then close. Then they waited till they heard singing. The congregation in church had started on the first hymn.

"Hurry. Go up to the gate," said Rhys ap Tudur to a man who was carrying carpenter's tools. "We'll be right behind you."

The pretend carpenter went up to the gate, and knocked.

"I've come to carry out emergency repairs to the woodwork in the King's Tower," said the man in his best English.

"General John de Massy sent for me."

The two guards looked at each other. They knew nothing of this. They opened the door an inch or two and peeped out. The carpenter looked honest enough, and was carrying a set of tools. Maybe the King's Tower was in need of repair. They'd heard that Henry IV was due to visit the castle quite soon.

"Come on in then," said one guard, opening the door wider.

"Forward, men, in the name of Owain Glyndŵr!" shouted Gwilym ap Tudur, and before the two guards knew what was happening, a wave of Welshmen came rushing towards them. When they were all inside, they bolted the gates and killed the two guards. The Welsh had taken the royal castle of Conwy!

John de Massy and his solders had a terrible shock when they returned from the Easter service. Henry IV's royal standards had disappeared from the castle, and fluttering in their place, were flags bearing pictures of four dragons.

"The banner of Owain Glyndŵr," whispered John de Massy. "The king will be beside himself when he hears that his castle has been captured by a small band of Welshmen!"

The Welsh held the castle for two months, but in the end they ran out of food. The king pardoned Rhys and Gwilym ap Tudur, and allowed them to lead the Welsh out of the castle. But on one condition. To save 32 of the men, 8 must be handed over to the English to be put to death.

Eight Welshmen were ready to die for the cause. They were hanged, as a warning to any Welshman who might consider joining the rebellion. Henry IV hoped to stem the flow of Welshmen who were flocking to Owain Glyndŵr.

But his plan failed. There were martyrs – men who were willing to die for the cause – who persuaded and inspired others to join Glyndŵr's rebellion. The flames of the rebellion were beginning to take hold in Wales.

Owain Glyndŵr's Diary

1401–1409

October 1401

This has been such a busy month, I've hardly had time to write. I've had to flee from place to place to avoid Henry IV's men.

We've had several near misses. When we were threatening Harlech castle, we heard that an army of 500 soldiers was on its way from Chester and had already reached Bala. So we left Harlech at speed. The soldiers' heads must be spinning!

News reached us that Henry's

Harlech Castle

troops had evicted the monks of Strata Florida Abbey, and housed both men and horses in the church. The king knows that the monks are among my keenest supporters, so he's taking revenge on them.

On October 9 1401, Llywelyn ap Gruffudd Fychan of Caio, one of my most dedicated supporters, was executed in Llandovery in front of the king. Poor Llywelyn! He was a generous and brave nobleman, who will be missed by everyone in the locality.

October 1401

The English have passed new laws. They are very racist. The Welsh no longer have any rights. We are not allowed to:

- hold important posts
- hold meetings
- be members of the garrison of an English castle
- be the patrons of poets
- bear arms on the highway or in any town or market
- buy land in England or in towns in Wales

The rebellion has obviously got to Henry IV!

2 November 1401

Today I led a Welsh army to the top of the old Celtic fort at Twtil, Caernarfon. I raised the banner of the golden dragon on high for everyone in the castle to see. Then we attacked the town and burnt it. Some of the soldiers barricaded themselves into the castle, so we couldn't get in. But one of my archers did manage to kill one very important person – the constable of the castle

April 1402

After a quiet winter, it was time to strike again. And what success we've had today! We captured Reginald Grey himself, Lord of Rhuthun and the Vale of Clwyd, my hellish neighbour! Some of my men wanted to hang him, but I wouldn't allow it. I need money to buy arms and supplies. So Reginald will be freed before the end of the year. But he'll have to pay a huge ransom – the extortionate sum of ten thousand marks!

Bryn Glas

22 June 1402

We won a massive victory today, at Bryn Glas near Knighton. It's near Offa's Dyke, and the English army had come over from Herefordshire. But in that army there were Welshmen who supported me. They killed their fellow-soldiers! By the time the battle came to an end there were hundreds of English dead.

We have one very important prisoner – Edmund Mortimer.

The battle took place on his land in Bryn Glas. He has a nephew, also called Edmund, who the Mortimer family believe is the rightful king of England. Our prisoner, Edmund Mortimer, has asked us to join forces against Henry IV. Things are looking up.

September 1402

Henry IV's army was on its way to fight us, but a violent storm drove them back. Henry thinks I'm a magician who can control the weather!

November 1402

Edmund Mortimer married my daughter Catrin today. It was a splendid ceremony, and Catrin looked lovely. Now that Edmund is a member of the family, he will surely remain loyal to me.

December 1402

Today Reginald Grey was released, though his servants tried to trick me! They brought a ransom of ten thousand marks, and asked me to hand over Reginald Grey.

"Hold on a minute," I said. "There's something wrong with these coins. They're not real. They're counterfeit!"

The cheating scoundrels! Well, I decided to teach them a lesson there and then.

"Reginald Grey's staying here," I said, "till you hand over double the ransom. That'll be twenty thousand marks."

The servants went off, and for several hours there was no sign of them. But back they came in the end – with twenty thousand marks!

July 1403

Things are going exceptionally well. 5,000 soldiers accompanied me to south Wales. First we went to Brecon and laid siege to the town. On the third of July I reached Llandovery, where many local noblemen hailed me as prince of Wales. On I went to Llandeilo, leaving 300 of my men to lay siege to Dinefwr and Dryslwyn castles.

What a fine place the Vale of Tywi is. There's plenty of food of all kinds: wheat, beans, honey, wine, and chickens too. The men have eaten well and enjoyed themselves.

I decided to follow the Vale of Tywi down as far as Carmarthen. We Welsh had not ruled Carmarthen for nearly three hundred years, since the coming of the Normans. But on the sixth of July 1403, my army managed to take the town and the castle of Carmarthen. As I write, the town and castle of Newcastle Emlyn are also under our command.

Sadly, I had bad news of my homes in Sycharth and Glyndyfrdwy. They were burnt to the ground, and two of my supporters killed.

October 1403
Good news from the town of Cydweli - Henry Dunn, with the aid of some soldiers from France and Brittany, has attacked Cydweli castle. I hope we'll have more help from France in the months to come.

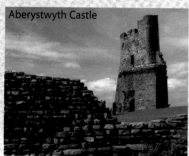
Aberystwyth Castle

Summer 1404
My army has taken Aberystwyth and Harlech castles. The town of Cydweli was again set on fire. My army now controls most of Wales.

A momentous event took place at Machynlleth – the first meeting of the parliament. We held important discussions on the future of Wales. Soon we'll have driven the English out of the country. Then we can start to build a new Wales. I've already appointed a chancellor and secretary. I have a coat of arms - the 4 lions of the prince of Gwynedd, and a privy seal, not unlike the King of England's seal. On the front there is a picture of me seated on my throne. On the back I'm on horseback with a helmet on my head.

But there was also an unfortunate incident during the session of parliament. One of my enemies, Dafydd Gam of Brecon, infiltrated the meeting with the intention of killing me. He was caught in time and thrown out.

Wonderful news from France – King Charles VI has promised support. Together we can defeat the English army. Henry IV will be shaking in his shoes!

Map of the Tripartite Indenture

28 February 1405
Today I was in Bangor where I signed a very important agreement – the Tripartite Indenture. The Indenture is an agreement between three people – myself, my son-in-law Edmund Mortimer, and Henry Percy, earl of Northumberland. Once we've got rid of Henry IV, we shall divide England and Wales into three new countries, as shown on the map. This will change the face of Britain.

I have invited four men from every commote (p.19) to attend another session of parliament, which on this occasion will be held in Harlech Castle. We need to discuss detailed plans for the future.

The whole family now lives in Harlech, my wife Marged, my children and grandchildren. It is both my home and my court.

August 1405
The French have arrived! Two and a half thousand Frenchmen landed at Milford Haven. They have already captured Haverfordwest, Cardigan and Carmarthen. They were meant to meet the English army near Worcester, but decided to turn back.

October 1405
We have just lost a battle to the English - the Battle of Pwllmelyn to the north of Usk. My brother Tudur was killed, and my son Gruffudd has been imprisoned. Dafydd Gam fought for the English. My men have vowed to punish him.

I'm afraid the tide is beginning to turn against us.

Winter 1408-9
These past years have been hard. I have lost many castles. The English have even recaptured Aberystwyth. The only areas where support is still strong are Meirionnydd, parts of north Ceredigion, and Caernarfon.

I don't know what will become of us. Harlech castle, our home, is under siege. A thousand Englishmen have been here since spring. The whole family is desperately worried. Edmund Mortimer, husband of my daughter Catrin, has died. The winters have been particularly hard to bear. We are close to starvation.

It's time for us men to try and escape. I'll have to leave my wife Marged, my daughters and granddaughters, in the castle.

I will not surrender to the English. I still hope to lead Wales to independence. I still have so many dreams.

A Letter to the King of France

31 March 1406

Pennal, near Machynlleth,
31 March 1406

Dear Charles VI, King of France,

We are in the sixth year of our reign here in Wales. Thank you very much for your support in sending soldiers to Milford Haven last August.

I am writing to ask for your support once more. As you know, we in Wales are forced to follow the English who support the Pope in Rome. But we would like to support Pope Benedict, who lives in Avignon, in your country. Could you help us do this?

We want to establish our own church in Wales. St Davids will be the headquarters of the Archbishop of Wales and the west of England too.

At the present time, the king's men are appointed to the most important posts in the church. Not one bishop can speak Welsh, so they can't talk to the people. I would like Pope Benedict to insist that every priest speak Welsh.

Would Pope Benedict also allow us to set up two universities in Wales – one in the north and one in the south? There is no university in Wales at the present time, and students from Wales must travel to England (Oxford or Cambridge), to France (Paris) or to Italy (Bologna) for their education.

I should be grateful if you would bring this letter to the notice of Pope Benedict.

Thank you

Owain Glyndŵr
Prince of Wales.

A Stay in Coety Castle

One day during Glyndŵr.'s Rebellion, a nobleman appeared at the gate of Coety Castle near Bridgend. He was tall and handsome, and very well dressed.

The man and his servant were looking for a night's lodging, and they were given a warm welcome by the owner of the castle, Sir Lawrence Berkrolles. In fact, they stayed on for several days, enjoying the finest food and wine.

'Thank you for your gracious welcome, sir,' said the nobleman to Sir Lawrence. 'But we must leave today.'

'Must you?' said Sir Lawrence. 'They say that that Welsh ruffian Owain Glyndŵr is in the area. King Henry's men are on his tail. Stay on for a day of two, to watch him being caught and join in the fun.'

'It's time Owain Glyndŵr was caught,' said the nobleman. 'He's been causing havoc in this area for long enough, so I hear. Still, I'm afraid we have to go.'

An hour later, the nobleman and his servant took their leave of Sir Lawrence at the gate of Coety castle. The nobleman extended his hand to Sir Lawrence and said softly, 'Owain Glyndŵr. takes your hand, and thanks you sincerely for the great kindness you showed him.'

Then Owain Glyndŵr. and his servant went away leaving a stunned and shocked Sir Lawrence Berkrolles. In fact they say he had such a shock, he never spoke again.

Owain Glyndŵr's Parliment in Machynlleth

Owain Glyndŵr

On the Berwyn, around 1516

The Abbot of Valle Crucis had got up very early. He decided to take a walk on the Berwyn mountains near Llangollen. It was a fine midsummer's day, and the Abbot was out of breath by the time he reached the summit.

Whom should he see walking there on his own, but Owain Glyndŵr.. He was dressed as if for battle, his armour glittering in the sun and his coat of arms shining.

'Ah, Abbot!' Owain greeted him. 'You have risen very early.'

'No, Lord Owain,' replied the Abbot. 'You are the one who rose early. You rose a hundred years before your time.' And with these words Owain Glyndŵr vanished.

Owain Glyndŵr's last years

Owain Glyndŵr. probably spent his last years as a fugitive - 'hiding in caves and forests on the mountainsides.'

His wife, Marged, two of their daughters and three little granddaughters were taken prisoner. His daughter Catrin and two of her daughters died in the Tower of London in 1413. They are buried in St Swithin's churchyard in London.

His son, Gruffudd, who had been taken prisoner at the Battle of Pwllmelyn, Usk, died in the Tower of London in 1411.

Owain is said to have disappeared on St Matthew's Day (21 September) in the year 1415. After that date we hear no more of him. He may have died around 1416 at the Herefordshire home of Alis, one of his daughters.

Owain Glyndŵr's memorial in Corwen

Why was Owain Glyndŵr important?

- ♛ He led a long rebellion against the English.
- ♛ For a while he managed to unite the whole of Wales.
- ♛ He had new and modern ideas regarding Wales. In the words of the Abbot of Valle Crucis, Owain Glyndŵr rose very early, too early for his time. This is when some of Owain Glyndŵr.'s dreams eventually became a reality:
- ♛ Universities for Wales – the first university in Wales was established in 1872 in Aberystwyth. Bangor and Cardiff followed in 1884.
- ♛ A Church for Wales – in 1920 the Church in Wales split from the Church of England.
- ♛ A Parliament for Wales – the Welsh National Assembly was set up in 1999.

INDEX

First published: September 2009
ⓟ original Welsh text: Gwasg Carreg Gwalch and Elin Meek
ⓟ English translation: Siân Lewis

ISBN: 978-1-84527-225-8

Published by Gwasg Carreg Gwalch, 12 Iard yr Orsaf,
Dyffryn Conwy, Cymru LL26 0EH.
tel: 01492642031
fax: 01492641502
e-mail: llyfrau@carreg-gwalch.com
website: www.carreg-gwalch.com

Text
Elin Meek

Editor
Gordon Jones

Photographs
Myrddin ap Dafydd 3, 6, 8-9, 12-3, 15-8, 23, 26, 29, 35-6, 38-40,
44-5, 47-9, 51, 53, 57-8, 61, 64-5, 73-7
Clybiau Ffermwyr Ifanc Cymru/Dimitris Legakis
    Photography 43tch&gch
Lyn Léwis Dafis 57 (Cofeb Gwenllïan): 64
Helen Emanuel Davies 43gdd
© Rachel Devine: main cover photograph
(www.ageoftheprinces.co.uk)
© Charles Hewitt/Picture Post/Getty Images 59
© Llyfrgell Genedlaethol Cymru (Peniarth 28) clawr, 18; (Rholyn
Ach Edward Almer) 32
Andrew Meek (catapwlt) 66
Photolibrary Wales/Keith Morris (Duffy) 39
Photolibrary Wales (Joe Calzhage; Ryan Giggs) 39
S4C/ J.O. Roberts 5 (Owain Glyndŵr); 71

Illustrations
Graham Howells 1, 7-9, 14, 16-7,19-23, 28-9, 32-3, 37, 41, 46, 52,
56, 60, 63-4, 69, 72, 77
Robin Lawrie 10, 12-13, 15, 24, 26-7, 30, 34, 40, 44, 50, 59, 62,
66-7, 68-9
Dai Owen 31, 45

Maps and charts
Charles Britton 2, 4, 5, 6, 11, 13, 19, 25-6, 42, 49, 54-5, 57, 70, 75

Design
Tanwen Haf

Thanks
Cyngor Rhondda Cynon Taf
Lyn Léwis Dafis
Helen Emanuel Davies
Dr John Davies
Gwasg Gomer
Gwyn Jenkins
Dewi Morris Jones
Mared Jones a Helen Edwards, Clybiau Ffermwyr Ifanc Cymru
D. Geraint Lewis
Hefin Mathias
Andrew Meek
J. O. Roberts
Alwyn J. Roberts
Michael Roberts
Sian Williams, Cyngor Sir Gwynedd

Published with the financial support
of the Welsh Books Council